Sylvia Gabet

vegetables
at their freshest and best

Photographs by Patrick Bauer

VEGETABLES
AT THEIR FRESHEST AND BEST

contents

Vegetables, simplicity itself!

Sedentary lifestyle, hectic pace of living and work, the tendency to cut corners—our modern diet is lacking in fresh vegetables, and children are the most deficient. Epidemiological studies and healthy-eating campaigns are there to remind us, however, that we should be eating five servings of fruit and vegetables a day. A basic principle for restoring vegetables' appeal: variety is as important as quantity. What a pleasure, then, to delight your tastebuds with the different flavors of vegetables, to feast your eyes on their gorgeous colors, or to cook them simply to set off meat or fish. Fresh vegetables also serve as signposts of the seasons: a cucumber salad takes us back to the sunny days of summer, while a leek and potato soup evokes cosy winter evenings by the fireside.

> A major source of nutrition
Vegetables are good for our health, not to mention our looks. Their nutritional and energy-giving properties are various. Vegetables contain vitamins from A to Z, as well as antioxidants; they are also rich in fiber, iron, and trace elements. Vegetables are crucial to our well-being: there's nothing like them for overcoming fatigue and raising our morale, and our bodies are grateful for it. What more could we ask for?

> Examining received wisdom
Vegetables are quick to prepare Chosen at the right time, certain vegetables don't even need peeling, and the recipes in this book always aim for the best "time spent in the kitchen" versus "taste result" ratio.

Vegetables aren't expensive If they're chosen in the right season. What's more, they're filling and allow you to you reduce your portions of meat—the costlier component of the meal. Good vegetables are not all necessarily stamped "organic," nor are they always more pricey. Study the labels and origins.

Vegetables taste good Although nowadays it's easier to buy most vegetables all year round, it's still true that they're more flavorful at the peak of their season. Get to know the different varieties of vegetables and when they're at their best. Have a look round the market stall, the store that sells early produce or the supermarket selling high-quality vegetables, and make them your sole supplier.

Vegetables are versatile Yes, beets need not be pickled and in a salad, and radishes can be cooked. Once again, variety is crucial for maximum appreciation of the incredible diversity of vegetables and the ways in which they can be prepared.

> Major principle of conservation—fresh means fresh
Fresh vegetables should be kept hanging around as little as possible. It's better to buy in small quantities and more often, rather than buying large amounts and letting them spoil. Fifty per cent of the vitamins are lost two days after the vegetables are picked.
So give free rein to your passion for vegetables, and vary the pleasures, the varieties and even the shapes. You've never tried carrot tagliatelle? To the vegetable shelves, everyone!

Vegetables, a user's guide

Season after season, vegetable after vegetable, discover 33 vegetables, from the best-known to the slightly unusual. Then make the acquaintance of some comeback vegetables, as well as salad leaves and condiments. Finally, browse through the appendices pages, where you'll find the best mixed-veg recipes, as well as a number of sauces and accompaniments to ring the changes.

> "User's guide" pages
• At the start of each section, you'll find a 'user's guide' double-spread introducing the vegetable with its different varieties and cooking methods.
• Using the calendar, check out the months during which the vegetable is at the height of its flavor.
• Next to the calendar, you'll find the number of "kcal per 100 g" (kilocalories per 100 g serving) and the nutritional components of the vegetable. I've made a point of emphasizing the ones readily linked to obvious benefits:
Vitamin C: Combats fatigue; helps in the formation of bones, teeth, and tissue.
Provitamin A: Antioxidant (protects the body against 'free radicals' which attack the nucleus of the cell); boosts our immune systems and protects skin against UV rays.
Vitamin B: Essential for the formation of new cells.
Vitamin E: Stimulates the immune system, anti-arthritic.
Magnesium: For nerves and muscles.
Fiber: Stimulates the digestive system.

> Recipe pages
The 'Vegetables, simplicity itself' sections offer between 6 and 10 recipes, each serving four, using simple preparation methods that make the most of the featured vegetable. You'll find both great classics and more-recent, original recipes.

In the recipe pages, our symbols show you four categories at a glance:

 A sure hit with children   Waistline-friendly

 Less than 20 minutes   Guaranteed to knock their socks off!

> Two big synoptique charts
Cooking methods and vegetables (see pp. 152–3): Depending on the vegetable in question, certain cooking methods are better than others. Here's a little memory-jogger to help you always get it right.
The seasons and vegetables (see pp. 154–5): For photocopying and tacking to the refrigerator, so it's always in sight.

VEGETABLES: AT THEIR FRESHEST AND BEST

spring

VEGETABLES

The world's "globe artichoke center" is Italy, where it is grown in most regions. France and Spain are close runners-up and, since the early 1990s, when it was introduced commercially into the US, the Salinas valley of California has become the main growing region here. The hairy "choke"—a reminder of the thistle from which it's descended—is simply the atrophied flower, and is not eaten. Artichokes can also be preserved in oil, and—at a pinch—stand up well to freezing.

Globe artichokes, a user's guide

**Medium to large globe artichoke
Small ("Poivrade" in France) artichoke**

Medium to large globe artichoke: Cook for around 20 minutes in boiling water; generally served with a vinaigrette (*see recipe p. 145*), but plenty of other accompaniments are also possible (*see p. 10*).

Small globe artichoke: Raw or cooked, its flavor and crunch work wonders in spring and summer meals. Its only drawback: rather fussy to prepare, with over 90 per cent of the vegetable being discarded—you're left with scarcely a mouthful!

> **Choosing for quality**
Choose really firm, compact and dense artichokes with tightly closed leaves.
Ideal size: Not too large, medium to small is better.
Bad sign: A limp stem and soft, blotchy leaves that don't snap easily indicate that the artichoke was picked too long ago.

> **Storage**
Best used on the day of purchase. Never store a cooked artichoke: it becomes toxic after 24 hours. Raw, it can be stored for 3–4 days in the fridge, or place the stalk in a glass of water—after all, the artichoke is a flower bud!

> **Preparation**

Large artichokes
Destalking The first step consists in breaking off the artichoke's stalk, rather than cutting it with a knife, in order to remove the woody fibers that extend all the way to the heart.
Boiling in water To keep them from discoloring, the professionals cook globe artichokes in a fond blanc (a large amount of water to which 2 oz all-purpose flour and 2 tablespoons of vinegar have been added). At home, plenty of salted water in a large stainless steel pan will do the trick. (Avoid aluminum or cast iron pans as they will discolor the vegetable.) Bring the water to a boil, then cook the artichokes for 20 minutes. They may discolor a bit, but their taste won't in any way be spoilt. Then simply drain the artichokes upside down, and let your guests get on with pulling off the leaves. You could also pull off the leaves and prepare the hearts in the kitchen.
Trimming If you are not cooking them in water, artichokes can be peeled as you would an orange, but using a larger knife. If you choose this method, remove the artichoke's leaves with a serrated knife, turning the vegetable as you do until you reach the heart.

Small artichokes
Trimming First cut off the stalk 1–1½ inches from the heart and peel it. Then remove the corolla from the first few outer leaves. Next, cut the leaves off horizontally halfway down, and finally slice the artichoke in two to reach the hairy choke, which should be removed. You can also "trim" the artichoke like peeling an orange, leaving fewer leaves than in the preceding manner.

Calendar

Energy

40 kcal per 100 g (artichokes are fairly high-energy due to their carbohydrate content).

Nutritional advantages

Rich in vitamins B, C, E and pro-vitamin A, as well as fiber and trace elements (including magnesium).

The artichoke's intense flavor marries well with the warm scents of spices such as curry powder, paprika, ginger, coriander seeds, and aniseed, as well as with all other spring vegetables. Small artichokes, delicious dipped in anchoïade (an anchovy, garlic, and olive oil purée), or simply munched with a sprinkling of salt or dunked in vinaigrette, are also marvelous cooked with tomatoes, onions, and diced bacon.

Globe artichokes, simplicity itself

 ### Medium artichokes with curry dip

> 4 medium artichokes > fromage blanc, beaten until smooth > curry powder > lemon juice > salt <

• Break the stalks off the artichokes and cook the artichokes for 20 minutes in plenty of boiling salted water. • Turn them upside down and drain well. • Prepare a dip with the fromage blanc: season with curry powder and lemon juice to taste and stir in with a spoon. • Enjoy your artichokes by dipping the leaves in the sauce, as with a vinaigrette.

➕ The flavor of curry powder harmonizes well with artichokes; if your children aren't fond of curry, substitute chives.

Globe artichoke 'nests'

> 4 artichokes > 8 oz fresh goat's cheese (or feta or Brousse) > chive vinaigrette > sea salt and freshly ground black pepper <

• Break the stalks off the artichokes and cook the globes for 20 minutes in plenty of boiling salted water, then drain them well. • Remove the leaves in the center, leaving most of the surrounding leaves for pulling and eating, until you reach the choke. • Remove the choke carefully using a teaspoon. • In a small bowl, beat and season your chosen cheese, then fill the artichoke hearts with the mixture. • Preheat the broiler. • Broil the globes for 5 minutes. • Before serving, spoon 1 tablespoon of chive vinaigrette over each globe artichoke nest.

➕ Another way to pull the leaves from the globes is by starting from the inside.

Minted small globe artichokes

> 6 small globe artichokes > 2 garlic cloves > 1 dozen mint leaves > olive oil for cooking > 4 tablespoons lemon juice > ½ cup dry white wine <

• Peel the artichokes, then cut them in half and remove the choke. • Finely chop the garlic and mint. • Heat the olive oil in a Dutch oven or flame-proof casserole dish and sauté the artichoke halves • Add the chopped garlic and mint, lemon juice, dry white wine and about ½ cup water. • Cover and cook for 30 minutes.

➕ A typically Italian dish, which can be served warm or cold as an appetizer, or as a delicious accompaniment to lamb.

Small globe artichokes with tomatoes and bacon

> 6 small globe artichokes > 4 tomatoes > 3 garlic cloves > 1 bunch salad onions > 3 carrots > olive oil for cooking > 1 cup smoked diced bacon > ½ cup dry white wine <

• Peel the globe artichokes, then cut them in half and remove the choke. • Quarter the tomatoes. Chop the garlic cloves. Peel the onions and carrots, and cut the carrots into sticks. • Heat the olive oil in a large pan and sauté the artichoke halves. • Add the vegetables and the diced bacon, dry white wine and ½ cup water. • Cover and cook for 30 minutes.

➕ These globe artichokes make a wonderful accompaniment for rabbit, roast chicken, grilled fish or scrambled eggs.

Griddled small globe artichokes with strips of ham

> 8 small globe artichokes > 2 garlic cloves
> 6 sprigs parsley > 2 slices ham (smoked, Serrano, etc.) > olive oil for cooking > chili powder <

• Peel the globe artichokes, cut in half and discard the choke, then cut them into thin strips. • Chop the garlic cloves and the parsley. • Cut the ham into thin strips. • Sauté the artichoke strips in olive oil in a griddle pan (or skillet or wok). • Sprinkle over the chopped garlic and parsley, a pinch of chili powder, and the strips of ham.

✚ No need to season, since the ham contributes enough salt. Serve as tapas with a glass of dry white wine, or as an appetizer.

Tagine of small globe artichokes, chicken, olives, and preserved lemon

> 4 chicken escalopes > 1 bunch salad onions
> 2 garlic cloves > olive oil for cooking > 8 small globe artichokes > 2 preserved lemons in brine > 16 pimento-stuffed black olives <

• Cut the chicken escalopes in half lengthwise, peel the onions and garlic cloves and crush the garlic. • Heat the olive oil in a skillet and sauté the escalope halves, onions and the crushed garlic. • Peel the globe artichokes, cut in half, remove and discard the choke, and add them to the pan. • Cook everything for 5 minutes. • Meanwhile, cut the lemons into small pieces. • Tip the contents of the pan into a tagine (or a Dutch oven or flameproof casserole), and add the diced lemon, 1 cup water and the olives. • Cover and simmer for 45 minutes.

✚ You'll find preserved lemons in Asian stores or on the "exotic products" shelf of your supermarket.

"Carpaccio" of small globe artichokes

> 6 small globe artichokes > 4 tablespoons lemon juice
> 4 tablespoons olive oil > 4 oz) piece of Parmesan cheese > sea salt and freshly ground black pepper <

• Peel the globe artichokes, cut in half and remove the choke, then cut them into very thin slices. • Arrange these slices on a large plate. • Sprinkle with lemon juice and olive oil. • Season with sea salt and pepper, and sprinkle with Parmesan shavings made with a vegetable peeler.

✚ Although the lemon juice slows down oxidation, this appetizer should be prepared at the last minute to prevent the globes from discoloring.

Cream of globe artichoke soup with aniseed

> 4 medium artichokes > 1 bunch of salad onions
> butter for cooking > 1 garlic clove, crushed
> 1 chicken bouillon cube, dissolved in 2 cups boiling water > 1 star anise > 1 cup crème fraîche (sour cream or thick, whole-fat yogurt) <

• Peel the globe artichokes, cut them in half and remove the choke, then cut the hearts into large pieces. • Peel the onions. • Melt a knob of butter in a large pan and sweat the onions and artichoke hearts for 5 minutes. • Add the crushed garlic, chicken bouillon and the star anise. • Cook for 20 minutes. • Fish out the star anise and 4 of the onions, which should be served whole, one per bowl, as a garnish. Blend the soup until smooth and stir in the crème fraîche.

✚ You can serve this creamy soup either hot or ice-cold as the mood takes you, or as dictated by the weather.

A member of the lily family (along with garlic, onions, and tulips), the underground root of the asparagus produces edible stalks known as "turions" in scientific quarters. Depending on the variety, asparagus spears never see the light of day (purple and white asparagus), or poke nothing but their tips above ground (violet-tipped asparagus—not to be confused with purple asparagus), or else spend a large part of their life above ground (green asparagus, which the sunlight fills with chlorophyll, spicing up its taste).

Asparagus, a user's guide

White asparagus
Purple variety 'Viola'
Purple-tinged asparagus
Green asparagus

White asparagus: Europeans prefer white asparagus; the Germans devour 72 tons of it every year, and many fans declare the best is from Bruchsal in Baden-Württemberg, southwestern Germany, while the French champion that from Argenteuil, near Paris, and Villelaure in Provence. Keep an eye open for it in the season as some of these spears, beloved of the Europeans, may have been graciously permitted to cross the Atlantic.

Purple asparagus: This variety—born in Italy but acclimatised across the Alps and even across the Atlantic—comes top of the "favorites" list for its sweet, almost slightly acid flavor.

Violet-tipped white asparagus: Popular in Europe.

Green asparagus: Its taste improves as it grows: the fattest stalks have a unique, spicy vegetable flavor. Green asparagus cooks twice as quickly as white spears of the same size: boiled, steamed, sautéed in butter, or griddled... it can even be enjoyed raw, cut into thin strips, and used as a dipper with fried eggs.

> **Choosing for quality**
Choose straight, smooth, unblemished spears with tightly closed tips and slightly moist stem ends.
Ideal size: As large as possible.
Bad sign: The stem end will give away a spear picked too long ago. If it is dry and woody, the asparagus is too old, and you'll have to trim it right back, only keeping the best part.

> **Storage**
As asparagus doesn't keep well, it's best to prepare it as soon after buying as possible. If you must keep it waiting, place the bottom of the spears in cold water, wrap the tops in a damp cloth, and never leave for longer than 3 days. Once cooked, consume without delay, as it oxidizes quickly.

> **Preparation**

White asparagus
Peeling Pare from the tip to the end with a vegetable peeler.
Cutting off the stem end Always more dry and woody than the stalk, this should be removed but not thrown away; it will lend taste to asparagus soup (see recipe p. 14).
Boiling In a small amount of salted water with stalks of the same size so they all cook in the same time (about 10 minutes). If need be, stagger their cooking times by about 3 minutes: add thick spears and woody ends to the water first, then medium spears 3 minutes later, then slender spears 3 minutes after that and cook for an additional 3 minutes. If you have, or wish to invest in, an asparagus pan, all the better, as the ends cook in the water while the heads gently cook in the steam. Save the cooking water and the woody ends for soup.
Eating with your fingers Good etiquette allows this, even in restaurants.

Green asparagus
Wash Green asparagus spears are so thin-skinned that there's no need to peel them, except perhaps a little toward the stalk end. Simply rinse them under running water without letting them soak.
Cooking Boil in water, or steam, or sauté in oil or butter.

Calendar

m a m j j

Energy
20 kcal per 100 g

Nutritional advantages
Contains high levels of vitamins C, E, B9 and provitamin A (fights fatigue, ageing and stress). Rich in fiber. Very low sodium content. Diuretic qualities.

Asparagus can be prepared with a simple vinaigrette, or plain melted butter and a few Parmesan shavings. An orange mousseline is also a superb way to highlight white asparagus. For the green spears, fresh black truffle is the ideal partner, even if it's reserved for special occasions.

Asparagus, simplicity itself

Asparagus in a tuna–tarragon sauce

> 24 asparagus stalks > 6 tarragon sprigs > 4 oz canned tuna in brine, drained weight > sherry vinegar > groundnut oil > 1 hard-cooked egg, finely grated > salt and freshly ground black pepper <

• Cut the ends off the asparagus and peel the stalks. • Cook the whole spears in a little boiling salted water, then drain them on an asparagus plate (or on a dish covered with paper towels). • If you want to prepare an asparagus soup, add the woody ends to the spears while they are cooking, and reserve the cooking water. • Chop the tarragon and break up the tuna with a fork. • Make the dressing by combining the vinegar, groundnut oil, salt and pepper, and add the chopped tarragon, tuna, and grated egg. • Gently mix everything together.

✚ This multiflavored dressing is a lovely accompaniment to the asparagus, served cold or warm (reheat for 30 seconds in the microwave).

Asparagus stalk soup

> 2 shallots > butter for cooking > Asparagus stalk ends, plus the asparagus cooking water > 2 tablespoons crème fraîche, sour cream, or thick yogurt <

• Peel the shallots and cut into rounds. • Melt a knob of butter in a pot, and sweat the sliced shallot. • Add the asparagus stalk ends and barely cover with the cooking water, then bring to a boil. • Simmer for 20 minutes. Blend until smooth and stir in the crème fraîche.

✚ A soup made from the peelings—no saving is too small, especially when it tastes so good!

You could also sprinkle this soup with a little crabmeat—the flavors complement each other perfectly.

 ## Pasta with green asparagus tips

> 1 bunch green asparagus > 4 oz piece Parmesan cheese > 4–5 basil leaves > 14 oz pasta > 4 tablespoons olive oil > sea salt and cooking salt <

• Cut off and reserve the tips of the asparagus. • The rest of the stalks can be used to make soup (*see recipe opposite*). • Shave the Parmesan with a vegetable peeler and chop the basil leaves. • Cook the pasta in plenty of boiling salted water. • 3 minutes before the end of cooking, add the asparagus tips, then drain everything thoroughly • Tip onto the serving plate, add the olive oil, and sprinkle with the Parmesan shavings and chopped basil leaves.

✚ Cooking the pasta and vegetables in the same pot saves time and washing up. If you wish, you can flavor the oil with a pinch of curry powder.

Green asparagus with butter and Parmesan

> 20 green asparagus stalks > 4 oz butter > 1¼ cups freshly grated Parmesan cheese > salt and freshly ground black pepper <

• Cut off the stalk ends of the asparagus and rinse the spears. • You can use the ends to make a soup (*see recipe opposite*). • Depending on their size, cook the whole spears for 5 to 10 minutes in a little boiling salted water, then drain them on an

asparagus plate (or a plate covered with paper towels). • Melt the butter with 1 tablespoon water in a pan. • Whisk until foamy. • Season with salt and pepper and pour over the asparagus tips, then sprinkle everything with Parmesan.

✚ A quintessentially Italian way to serve asparagus, and *simplissimo* to boot!

Purée of green asparagus with sesame seeds

> 3 lb green asparagus > 1 medium-sized potato > 1 shallot > butter for cooking > 2 chicken bouillon cubes, dissolved in 1¼ pints boiling water > 2 tablespoons sesame seeds <

• Wash the asparagus spears and cut into quarters. • Peel and slice the potato. • Peel the shallot, slice and sweat in a pan with a small knob of butter until soft. • Add the asparagus spears, potato slices and the chicken bouillon. • Bring to a boil and cook over a low heat for 10 minutes. • Meanwhile, toast the sesame seeds in a dry skillet (30 seconds is long enough). • Purée the asparagus and potato mixture in a blender until smooth. • Serve sprinkled with the sesame seeds.

✚ This purée is a true delicacy. It is delicious served with roast chicken, veal, or even soft-cooked eggs.

 ## Green asparagus with coriander cream

> 20 green asparagus spears > 1 tablespoon coriander seeds > ¾ cup light cream > 2 tablespoons lemon juice > salt and freshly ground black pepper <

• Cut the stalk ends off the asparagus and rinse the spears. • You can use the stalk ends to make soup (*see recipe opposite*). • Depending on their size, cook the whole spears for 5 to 10 minutes in a little boiling salted water, then drain them well on an asparagus plate (or a plate covered with paper towels). • Grind the coriander seeds. • Tip the ground spice into a skillet, stir in the cream and bring to a boil. • Cook for 2 minutes. • Season to taste with salt and pepper, then stir in the lemon juice. • Serve in a sauce boat as an accompaniment to the asparagus.

✚ A highly aromatic variant of the classic lemon-flavored cream.

 ## White asparagus with orange mayonnaise

> 20 white asparagus spears > 1 orange > 1 lemon > mayonnaise (*see recipe p. 147*) <

• Cut the stalk ends off the asparagus and rinse the spears. • You can use the stalk ends to make soup (*see recipe opposite*). • Depending on their size, cook the whole spears for 5 to 10 minutes in a little boiling salted water, then drain them on an asparagus plate (or a plate covered with paper towels). • Finely grate the orange rind to obtain ½ teaspoon zest, and squeeze the orange to obtain 1 tablespoon juice. • Squeeze the lemon to obtain 1 teaspoon juice. • Prepare a classic mayonnaise with grapeseed oil, and season it with the orange and lemon juice and the orange zest. • Serve with the asparagus.

✚ If you're looking for a speedier version of this dish, substitute mascarpone for the mayonnaise.

Peas and English broad beans or fava beans need to be shelled—broad beans must also be skinned—but their cousins, snow peas, are prepared in a flash. The latter are classified as a green vegetable, while the former belong to the family of legumes. When young and tender, however, broad beans and peas can truly pass for fresh green vegetables.

Broad/fava beans and edible-pod peas, a user's guide

Fresh and dried broad beans
English broad beans and fava beans
Peas
Snow peas

English broad beans: can be found in the US but usually only in farmers' markets. Some seed catalogs carry the seed, so watch for the classic English variety 'Windsor.' **Baby broad beans,** picked a third of the way through their development, are still small and tender. They are shelled, blanched, then eaten with a knob of butter. Three-quarters of the way through development, broad beans are termed "fresh" (recognizable from their green pods). Left any longer, the pods dry on the stalk and turn brown. They are then knocked off the plant to obtain dried broad beans. **Fava beans** are mainly used dried but fresh ones can be found in the spring.

Fresh peas: Usually sold in their pods, stores sometimes sell them in bags, already shelled. Frozen peas are an excellent alternative when fresh are not available. Fresh peas have nothing in common with canned ones, and should preferably be steamed or sautéed in oil or butter so that their flavor and vitamins are not diluted in water.

Snow peas: an edible-pod pea. Simply rinse and steam or sauté for 3 minutes to preserve their delicate flavor and vitamins. Eaten whole, in Britain and Europe the variety is called mangetout (literally, "eat all").

Fresh broad beans, baby broad beans, fava beans, peas

> **Choosing for quality**

Choose bright green, firm, unblemished pods.
Ideal size: Pods that are less bulging will contain smaller, more tender beans. For peas, choose pods that are well filled out.
Bad sign: Dry, yellowed pods betray beans that have reached maturity. Although no longer fresh, they are still edible, but very "starchy". Garden peas that have reached this stage are not worth bothering with.

> **Storage**

No longer than 2 days in their pods, and once they've been shelled, cook immediately. It's worth mentioning that frozen young broad beans are excellent.

> **Preparation**

Shelling Broad beans, baby broad beans and fresh peas must be shelled. The pods of freshly picked baby broad beans and peas can be used in soup.
Skinning Once broad beans have been shelled, their light-colored skin, which grows thick over time, should be removed. (Baby broad beans need not be skinned.) To skin broad beans, plunge them first for 1 minute in very salty boiling water. Drain, then refresh in iced water. Once cool, pinch them between your thumb and finger and the skins should slip off easily. Prepared in this way, broad beans are cooked sufficiently to be eaten straight away.

Edible-pod peas

> **Choosing for quality**

Choose vivid green pods, with very little seed development. The pod should snap crisply when bent.
Ideal size Select pods that are not too long.
Bad sign Avoid bulging pods and seeds that have already grown.

> **Storage**

No more than 2 days in the vegetable compartment of your fridge.

> **Preparation**

Washing A light rinse will chase away any "intruders". If they are very fresh, just top and tail them. A little way into the season some may need "stringing".

Calendar	Energy	Nutritional advantages
	Fresh and baby broad beans supply 35 kcal per 100g; dried broad beans supply 250 kcal. per 100g; peas supply 67 kcal per 100g	These vegetables are good sources of protein, carbohydrate, vitamin C, iron and cellulose.

Fresh broad beans are steamed, or sautéed in a Dutch oven or pan like a green vegetable. Savory, thyme and mint are the herbs that flatter them, as does cumin. Fresh garden peas, as well as fresh broad/fava beans, are delicious with diced bacon, carrots and scallions. Add a few edible-pod peas to round things out, and spring is in the air!

Broad/fava beans and edible-pod peas

Salad of fresh (baby) broad beans and radishes with sheep's milk cheese

> 1¾ lb broad/fava beans or baby broad beans in their pods (or 10 oz shelled) > 1 bunch radishes > 2 shallots > fresh mint leaves > 4 oz sheep's-milk cheese > vinaigrette (see recipe p. 145) <

• Shell and skin the broad beans (if using baby broad beans, simply shell). Blanch in boiling water for 3 minutes. • Top and tail the radishes and slice them into rounds; chop the shallots and mint leaves and cut the cheese into thin slices. • Prepare a classic vinaigrette. • Tip the beans into a salad bowl and add the sliced radish, chopped shallot, and cheese slices. • Pour over the vinaigrette, toss everything carefully and sprinkle with chopped fresh mint.

✚ If the broad beans are on the large size, blanch them for 5 minutes instead of 3.

Baby broad beans with bacon and marrow

> 2½ lb baby broad beans in their pods (or 14 oz shelled) > 1 shallot > the marrow from a marrowbone (decorticated by the butcher) or 2 tablespoons olive oil > 1 cup diced smoked bacon > 1 thyme sprig > 1 vegetable bouillon cube <

• Shell the baby broad beans. • Peel and chop the shallot. • Melt the marrow or heat the olive oil in a skillet. • Add the chopped shallot, diced bacon, thyme, bouillon cube and ¾ cup water. • Bring to a boil. Add the broad beans, bring back to a boil and cook for 3 minutes (the broad beans should remain slightly crisp).

✚ Serve as a side dish with lamb chops, shoulder of lamb or roast rack of lamb.

Cream of broad bean/fava bean soup with gingerbread croutons

> 2½ lb broad beans in their pods (or 14 oz shelled) > 1 potato > 2 cups light cream > 1 vegetable bouillon cube > 2 slices gingerbread > 1 oz butter <

• Shell and skin the broad beans. • Set aside about 20 empty pods. • Peel the potato and cut it into pieces about the size of the beans. • Place the broad beans, potato and reserved pods in 2 cups water. Add the cream and bouillon cube, bring to a gentle boil and cook for 10 minutes. • Blend until smooth and serve accompanied by the gingerbread, cut into dice and fried for several minutes in the butter until crisp.

✚ This soup is delicious served either hot or ice-cold.

Pasta with baby broad/fava beans, peas, green asparagus, and Brousse cheese

> 1 dozen green asparagus spears > 10 oz baby broad beans in their pods (or 1 cup shelled) > 10 oz peas in the pod (or ¾ cup shelled) > 12 basil leaves > 14 oz pasta > butter for cooking > 7 oz Brousse (a Provençal fresh goat's or ewe's-milk cheese) > 4 tablespoons crème fraîche, or thick yogurt > grated Parmesan cheese <

• Rinse the asparagus and peel if necessary, then cut into thirds. • Shell the broad beans and peas.

Hot tip

Snow peas: neatly packaged, already picked over, ready to plunge in boiling salted water and be eaten plain, simply seasoned with some sea salt.

• Chop the basil leaves. • Cook the pasta in plenty of boiling water. Ten minutes before the end of cooking, add the peas and broad beans, then 5 minutes later, the asparagus pieces. • Drain the pasta and vegetables and sauté for 5 minutes in a skillet with the butter to drive off the excess moisture. • Transfer everything to the serving dish and add the Brousse and the crème fraîche. • To finish, sprinkle over with the chopped basil and grated Parmesan.

 You can substitute ricotta for the Brousse cheese, possibly adding a hint of garlic to the pan when sautéing the pasta.

Cream of pea and snow pea soup

> 1½ lb peas in the pod > 10 oz snow peas > 1 leek > 1 onion > butter for cooking > 3 chicken bouillon cubes, dissolved in 6 cups boiling water > ¾ cup light cream <

• Shell the peas. • Rinse the snow peas and top and tail if necessary. • Wash the leek and cut into rounds; peel the onion and slice into rounds. • Melt a knob of butter in a skillet and sweat the leek and onion. • Once they are translucent, add the peas, followed by the hot chicken bouillon. • Cook for 15 minutes. • Blend in an electric blender and stir in the cream, then blend again until smooth.

You may wish to skim off a handful of peas and snow peas with a slotted spoon after they have cooked for 5 minutes. They'll still be crisp, and you can then add them to the soup as a garnish just before serving.

Fresh peas, early carrots, onions, and bacon

> 4 lb fresh peas in the pod > 1 bunch salad onions > 4 carrots with tops on > 1½ cups diced bacon > 1 small lettuce heart, chopped > 1 sprig parsley > 1 sprig mint > 1 teaspoon sugar > salt and freshly ground black pepper <

• Shell the peas. • Peel and half the onions, peel the carrots but leave whole with about an inch of stem. • Render the bacon in its own fat in a skillet; add the onions, lettuce heart, carrots, peas, parsley, and mint. • Sprinkle with sugar, stir, pour in ¾ cup water and season to taste. • Cover and cook for 20 minutes.

Cook for 10 minutes longer if you prefer your peas more tender. Serve with meat or fish.

Snow peas, carrot, tomato, apple, and pine nut salad

> 7 oz snow peas > 2 carrots > 1 Granny Smith apple > 2 tomatoes > balsamic vinegar > hazelnut oil > handful of pine nuts or crushed hazelnuts > salt <

• Rinse the snow peas and top and tail if necessary. • Peel the carrots and cut lengthways into sticks. • Peel and slice the apple. • Rinse the tomatoes, then slice into rounds. • Blanch the snow peas for 3 minutes in boiling salted water, then lift them out with a slotted spoon and refresh them in ice water. • Blanch the carrots for 3 minutes in the same boiling water. • Prepare a vinaigrette in a salad bowl with the balsamic vinegar and hazelnut oil. • Add the peas, apple, tomato slices, and carrot sticks. • Toss everything together and add a handful of pine nuts or hazelnuts.

A stunning savory-sweet salad, which looks just as good as it tastes.

"What? I'm King of France and I'm not allowed to eat spinach?" Louis XVIII is said to have exclaimed, outraged, to physicians who forbade him the vegetable on account of his gout. The idea of being deprived of spinach was intolerable! Nowadays, spinach is less popular than it was in the 18th century, although it's a highly flavorful vegetable, packed with nutrients (even if—contrary to a misapprehension spread by the creator of Popeye—it contains very little iron). Its cousin, New Zealand spinach (Tetragonia), is starting to appear in the market, and is mainly eaten raw.

Spinach, a user's guide

Spinach
New Zealand spinach (Tetragonia)

Spinach: The young shoots are eaten—preferably raw—in salads, while the large, coarser leaves are lightly cooked.

New Zealand spinach: Despite its name, this vegetable is actually a close relation of the ice plant (Mesembryantheum). Its arrow-shaped leaves have their own characteristic strong taste. It is best eaten raw, like young spinach shoots. Tetragonia is often substituted for spinach during the summer months.

> **Choosing for quality**
Choose spinach with fine, large, unblemished, dark-green leaves.
Ideal size: None, but choose leaves of the same size for preference, so they all cook in the same time.
Bad sign: If the ribs are dry, it means that the spinach was picked too long ago and it will be tough.

> **Storage**
As with salad greens, fresh spinach can only be kept for a short while. Whatever you do, don't store cooked spinach, owing to the formation of toxic nitrites.

> **Preparation**
Washing and removing tough ribs Carefully wash the spinach leaf by leaf then spin it; cut out the thickest ribs.
Cooking know-how Par-cook without any additional water, rather than boiling hard, which will only cause the vast bulk of your harvest or purchase to disappear. One par-cooking technique consists of allowing the spinach to "wilt", in other words, more or less melt down in its own liquid, while you turn it constantly in a pan over medium heat. The other solution is to cook the spinach Italian style, in a skillet in a drizzle of olive oil, stirring it with a fork speared with a clove of garlic to impart a very gentle garlicky flavor to the greens.

Calendar	Energy	Nutritional advantages

Energy
A diet-friendly vegetable.

Nutritional advantages
4 to 6 mg of pro-vitamin A per 100 g (a record!), but also generous amounts of vitamin C and minerals (calcium, zinc, copper, manganese, etc.)

Spinach harmonizes brilliantly with cream and butter, of course, but also with veal, poultry, fish and eggs. Moreover, spinach makes a wonderful ingredient in numerous stuffings.

Spinach, simplicity itself

Spinach, Italian-style

> 2 lb spinach > olive oil or butter for cooking > 1 garlic clove > lemon juice > 1 small pot plain low fat yogurt (optional) <

• Pick over the spinach, cutting out the coarse ribs, and wash and spin the leaves. • Heat a drizzle of olive oil or a small knob of butter in a skillet and add the spinach leaves. • Spear the garlic clove with a fork and use to stir the spinach. • When the spinach has wilted, add the lemon juice and the yogurt (if using). • Mix together and serve immediately.

+ A cooking method which takes 5 minutes at the most, which makes up for the slightly drawn-out step of picking-over the greens.

Pasta with spinach, diced bacon, and cherry tomatoes

> 4 large handfuls fresh spinach leaves > 1 cup diced smoked bacon > $\frac{1}{2}$ cup dry white wine > 8 cherry tomatoes, halved > 14 oz pasta > 1 cup grated Parmesan (or pecorino) cheese > olive oil > salt and freshly ground black pepper <

• Pick over the spinach leaves. • Brown the diced bacon in a large pan; pour in the white wine and reduce until all the moisture has evaporated. • Now add the spinach and allow to wilt, stirring constantly for 5 minutes. • Lastly, add the cherry tomatoes, and season with pepper but not salt. • In another pan, cook the pasta in plenty of boiling salted water until tender; drain well and tip the hot pasta into the pan. Stir well to mix. • Sprinkle over with the grated cheese and drizzle with a little olive oil just before serving.

+ You can also make this recipe with arugula, a perfect substitute for the fresh spinach leaves.

Country spinach soup

> 2 lb spinach > 1 garlic clove > butter for cooking > 4 eggs > 4 slices smoked ham > salt and freshly ground black pepper <

• Wash the spinach and cut out any coarse ribs, tear the larger leaves into pieces; dry in a salad spinner. • Crush the garlic clove. • Melt a knob of butter in a skillet, wilt the spinach and add the garlic, salt, and pepper. • Heat 4 cups water in a pan and tip in the spinach. • Cook gently for 20 minutes. • Meanwhile, poach the eggs. • Serve the soup with a poached egg and a slice of ham at the bottom of each bowl.

+ You could also blend this rustic soup, and garnish with a few slices of toasted baguette.

Young spinach and almond croquettes

> 1 lb young spinach > 1 onion > 1 garlic clove > 2 eggs > butter for cooking > 4 tablespoons milk > 1½ cups breadcrumbs, made from stale bread > 1 cup slivered almonds > 1 pinch nutmeg > salt and freshly ground black pepper <

• Wash the spinach and discard the ribs. • Blanch for 3 minutes in boiling salted water, then drain in a colander, pressing hard to extract as much water as possible. • Peel and finely slice the onion; crush the garlic in the garlic press, and beat the eggs. • Melt some butter in a pan and sauté the sliced onion until it has softened and colored slightly. • Place the well-drained spinach in a bowl and add the onion, garlic, milk, eggs, breadcrumbs, almonds,

Hot tip

New Zealand spinach in a Caesar dressing with anchovies and Parmesan—the gutsy flavors harmonize superbly.

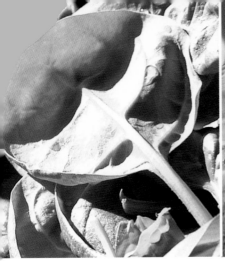

the onion, garlic, milk, eggs, breadcrumbs, almonds, nutmeg, salt, and pepper. • Mix well. • Shape into small croquettes and brown in butter for 2 minutes on each side in the pan in which the onion was cooked.

✛ For an equally delicious dish, substitute pine nuts or hazelnuts for the almonds.

Spinach and Rocamadour cheese custards

> 7 oz spinach > 1¾ cups milk > 1 cup light cream > 3–4 slices white sandwich bread > 4 Rocamadour cheeses (small goat's cheeses) > 3 eggs, beaten > 1 pinch grated nutmeg > salt and pepper <

• Preheat the oven to 350°F. • Wash the spinach and discard any coarse ribs. • Blanch for 3 minutes in boiling salted water, then drain in a colander, pressing hard to extract as much water as possible. • Heat the milk and cream together until warm. Crumble the bread, place in a bowl and soak with the milk mixture, then add the spinach and cheeses. • Blend well, then stir in the eggs and nutmeg. Season and mix well. • Pour the mixture into ramekins and bake in the preheated oven in a water bath (place ramekins in a roasting tin filled with hot water half way up their sides) for 20 minutes.

✛ Serve these baked savory custards with a salad of tomatoes or fresh herbs.

New Zealand spinach salad with Caesar dressing

> 1 lb New Zealand spinach > 2 garlic cloves > 4 anchovy fillets > garlic croutons > vegetable oil for cooking > 1 teaspoon mustard > 4 tablespoons lemon juice > 4 tablespoons olive oil > 1 teaspoon Worcestershire sauce > Parmesan cheese shavings > sea and freshly ground black pepper <

• Pick through, wash and spin the spinach. • Crush the garlic and mash the anchovy fillets. • Brown the garlic croutons in hot vegetable oil for 5 minutes. • Place the crushed garlic in a salad bowl and add the mustard, lemon juice, olive oil, Worcestershire sauce, and mashed anchovies; season to taste with salt and pepper. • Toss everything well and serve with the Parmesan shavings and garlic croutons.

✛ California Caesar salad is normally prepared with romaine, that long-leaved lettuce variety, similar to a cos lettuce. To serve as a main dish, add one soft-boiled egg per person.

Spinach and goat's cheese pie

> 3 lb spinach > 1 oz butter > 1 garlic clove > 2 fresh goat's cheeses (approx. 8 oz total weight) > 2 ready-made pizza bases > 2 tablespoons pine nuts > vegetable oil > salt and freshly ground black pepper <

• Preheat the oven to 400°F. • Wash the spinach and discard any coarse ribs. • Spin, and prepare Italian style with butter and garlic (see recipe p. 20). • Season with salt and pepper. • Chop the goat's cheeses into pieces. • Place one of the pizza bases in a pie dish. • Arrange the spinach on top and sprinkle with the pieces of cheese. • Sprinkle with pine nuts and cover with the second pizza base. • Brush with oil and cut a cross in the center with the tip of a sharp knife to allow the steam to escape. • Bake in the preheated oven for 40 minutes.

✛ The only difference between a pie and a tart is one less layer of dough. If you decide to leave off the top layer, watch closely so that the cheese doesn't burn. To ring the changes, substitute Gouda or aged Mimolette for the goat's cheese.

An ancient root vegetable, radishes are depicted in the hieroglyphs of the temple of Karnak, Egypt. Pink, white or black, each belongs to a different season. Pink radishes are the harbingers of spring, the season in which they are particularly sweet and flavorful. Long white radish is a summer vegetable, while long black radishes are fall and winter vegetables. The least nutrient-rich of the root vegetables, radishes nevertheless supply their fair share of minerals.

Radishes,
a user's guide

Pink radish
White radish
Black radish

Pink radish: A spring radish, this is the sweetest of them all. Raw or cooked, its crunch and color make it a children's favorite. It's only when it hasn't been picked at the peak of its ripeness and is left in the ground too long that the sulfurous, piquant substances contained in mustard, are formed. We distinguish between the "mid-long white-tipped pink" and the "pink and round all over", but their taste is much the same.

White radish: A summer radish with a more pronounced taste.

Black radish: A fall and winter radish with an often piquant taste: for adult palates only.

> **Choosing for quality**
Choose only firm, smooth radishes free from cracks and blemishes, with an attractive bouquet of dark-green tops in the case of the pink variety.
Ideal size: Not too big—medium-sized is best.
Bad sign: Too big—this means that the radishes have been in the ground for far too long. They are likely to pack a bit of a "bite", and may well be mushy or hollow.

> **Storage**
Young pink radishes are delicate and are best stored for no more than 3 days in the vegetable compartment of your refrigerator. White or black radishes are sturdier and can be kept a bit longer.

> **Preparation**
Washing Young pink radishes should not be peeled, but simply rinsed and drained. You then need only cut off the rootlet and most of the tops, leaving a bit of a 'tail' to grab hold of.
Peeling Black and white radishes must be peeled with a vegetable peeler. Only peel the part you'll be using—the remainder will keep a lot better with its skin left on.

Calendar

Energy
20 kcal per 100 g (has the lowest calorie count of the root vegetables).

Nutritional advantages
Radishes are rich in iodine and iron, as well as vitamins B and C. The tops of pink radishes contain an appreciable amount of pro-vitamin A; black radishes are rich in fiber.

The classic way to eat pink radishes is to dip them in salt and a knob of butter, but they can also be cooked! They make a delicious vegetable accompaniment for fish, amongst other things. Black radishes and white radishes are served cooked like turnips, or raw and finely grated Japanese-style, in the shape of very thin vermicelli, for instance.

Radishes, simplicity itself

'Salad Niçoise' with lots of pink radishes

> 1 bunch pink radishes > 1 carrot > 4 tomatoes > 2 salad onions > 4 mushrooms > ½ green pepper > balsamic vinegar > olive oil > 4 hard-cooked eggs > 1 handful fresh herbs, finely chopped > toasted slices of bread > tapenade > salt and freshly ground black pepper <

• Rinse the vegetables. • Cut the radishes and carrot into rounds, slice the tomatoes, onions, and mushrooms, and cut the pepper into strips. • Prepare a vinaigrette with the balsamic vinegar and olive oil. • Cut the hard-boiled eggs into quarters. • Mix the vegetables in a salad bowl, pour over the vinaigrette and arrange the eggs on top, then sprinkle with the finely chopped fresh herbs. • Serve accompanied with slices of toast spread with tapenade.

+ In the spring, I always keep pre-cut pink radish rounds covered in plastic wrap, ready to scatter over my mixed salads.

Fricassée of pink radishes

> 2 bunches pink radishes > butter or olive oil for cooking > sea salt <

• Trim and wash the radishes. • Reserving the tops if you want to make a radish-top soup (*see recipe opposite*). • Drain the radishes well, then turn them in a pan in hot butter or oil for 10 minutes; they should remain slightly crunchy. • Season with sea salt to give this radish fricassée even more crunch.

+ Serve as an accompaniment to fish or meat (roast chicken or rabbit), placing the radishes in the cooking juices of the meat for the last 10 minutes of cooking.

 ### Radish-top soup

> 2 bunches pink radishes > 1 oz butter > 1 tablespoon cornstarch (optional) > 2 tablespoons thick crème fraîche, yogurt, or sour cream (use low fat varieties if you are watching your waistline) > 4 mint leaves, finely chopped > salt and freshly ground black pepper <

• Cut the tops off the radishes, wash them and dry in a salad spinner. • Melt the butter in a pan and sauté the tops for 3 minutes until the leaves wilt. • Add water to cover, season with salt and pepper, bring to a boil and cook for 5 minutes (no longer in order to preserve the vitamins). • You can thicken this soup with the cornstarch if you prefer. • Purée in a blender until smooth and add the crème fraîche. • Mix until thoroughly combined. • Serve topped with the finely chopped mint leaves.

+ You can make a soup of mixed-greens by substituting the tops of one bunch of the radishes with the same quantity of fresh spinach leaves.

 ### Cream of pink radish soup

> 1 bunch pink radishes > 2 shallots > ¾ cup dry white wine > 2 cups light cream > salt <

• Trim and wash the radishes. • Reserving the tops if you want to make radish-top soup (*see previous recipe*). • Quarter the radishes and blanch in boiling salted water for 5 minutes, then drain. • Peel and thinly slice the shallots. • Pour the white wine into a pan, add the sliced shallots and reduce until the liquid has completely evaporated. • Add the cream and bring to a boil; remove from the heat and allow

Black radishes cut into rounds can take the place of bread as an appetizer, spread with tapenade, anchoïade (anchovy paste), Roquefort butter, cream cheese with a pinch of curry powder…

to cool slightly before whizzing in a blender until smooth. • Lastly, add the radish quarters and blend once again.

+ Serve this soup as a first course, followed by fish or poultry.

White radish confit

> 1 white radish > butter for cooking > 2 teaspoons sugar > 1 chicken bouillon cube, dissolved in 1 cup boiling water > salt and freshly ground black pepper <

• Peel the radish and slice into thin rounds. • Melt a knob of butter in a skillet and sauté the radish until golden. • Season with salt and pepper to taste and add the sugar and the chicken bouillon. • Cook over a low heat for 30 minutes.

+ This radish confit makes the perfect partner for duck. If you're not averse to a slightly richer dish, you can stir 2 oz butter into the sauce just before serving.

 ## Black radish salad with soy sauce

> 1 black radish > 1 teaspoon salt > 1 tablespoon sherry vinegar > 1 tablespoon Japanese soy sauce > 4 tablespoons light vegetable oil (grapeseed, sunflower or groundnut) > freshly ground black pepper <

• Peel and finely grate the black radish. • Prepare a vinaigrette dressing by mixing together the salt, freshly ground black pepper to taste, sherry vinegar, soy sauce, and oil, in that order. • Arrange the grated radish on a plate and sprinkle with the vinaigrette dressing just before serving.

+ For a pretty mixture of colors, add some corn salad (lamb's lettuce) and carrot sticks to this Japanese-style salad; or to give it a more interesting consistency, jazz it up with large peeled shrimp, strips of smoked salmon, fresh sashimi-style salmon, or pan-fried scallops.

Marinated salmon and black radish appetizers

> 1 fresh salmon fillet > 3 dill sprigs > 1 black radish > 2 tablespoons lemon juice > 2 tablespoons olive oil > 1 tablespoon crème fraîche, thick yogurt or sour cream > salt and freshly ground black pepper <

• Cut the salmon fillet into strips. • Finely chop the dill to obtain about 1 tablespoon. • Peel the radish and slice into 8 rounds. • Combine the lemon juice, olive oil, chopped dill, salt and pepper on a plate, turn the salmon strips in it, and marinate for 30 minutes. • Remove the salmon from the marinade and mix gently with the crème fraîche. • Arrange the salmon strips on top of the radish rounds.

+ You can serve these with drinks, or as an appetizer garnished with a mixture of fresh chervil and chives.

Black radish chips

> 1 black radish > oil for deep-frying > salt <

• Peel the radish and shave into thin rounds. • Cook in a deep-fryer for 10 minutes and drain on paper towels. • Salt as you would potato chips and serve as an appetizer with drinks.

+ Season with sea salt for even more crunch. Delightful!

summer

Long, round, purplish-black or marbled—eggplants are the big stars of summer cuisine. Always cooked, they can be served either hot or cold. The skin—smooth and sweet, almost lacquered in appearance—is eaten or not, depending on the recipe. The eggplant is a sun worshiper: it needs a minimum nighttime temperature of 60°F, so its thrives best in southern Mediterranean-type climates.

Eggplants, a user's guide

'Black Beauty' eggplant
'Black Bell' eggplant
'Zebra' Purple and white striped eggplant
Dourga White eggplant
Mini eggplant

'Black Beauty' eggplant: The traditional very dark purple, pear-shaped variety of eggplant, parent of many new varieties.

'Black Bell' eggplant: Medium to large, Round-oval, glossy almost black—the traditional Italian type.

'Zebra' striped eggplant: Another Italian-style variety, around 6–8 inches long with a delightfully marked skin, a truly delightful vegetable.

Dourga White eggplant: more ivory-colored than white the skin is thin and the flesh tender and seldomly bitter.

Mini eggplant: Takes just a few seconds in the microwave (with 1 tablespoon water) to cook. A drizzling of olive oil, a pinch of sea salt, and you're in heaven!

> ## Choosing for quality
Eggplants should be firm, smooth-skinned and unblemished. The stalk should be a fine light-green color, full of sap and quite spiny, proof of the fruit having been picked before it ripened, as should be the case. Eggplants are often imported and, as they are seasonal, their price fluctuates.
Ideal size: Not too big, so it won't contain too many seeds, or have too thick a skin (important if you're not going to peel it).
Bad sign: A dry stalk means that the eggplant is not spanking fresh. A dark-green stalk means that the eggplant was picked too late, and may well be bitter.

Storage
> No particular pains need be taken, since their thick skin serves as protection. They can be kept well for 2–3 days in the vegetable compartment of the refrigerator.

Preparation
> *Washing* If eating them with their skin, wash the eggplants, taking care to remove the stalk only after washing, so they don't absorb lots of water.
Peeling To peel or not to peel? If you want to make the most of the eggplant's tenderness, you'll have to peel it, whereas for some recipes you prefer to let the skin hold the slices together.
How to go about it With a vegetable peeler, taking care to cook the eggplant immediately afterward so that it doesn't discolor.
Salting and draining This trick stops the eggplant from soaking up too much oil during cooking, and removes any bitterness in the vegetable. Simply cut the eggplants into slices, sprinkle with cooking salt on both sides and place them in a colander. Rinse under running water after 30 minutes, then blot dry with paper towels.
Cooking Be aware that eggplants don't take kindly to boiling, which emphasizes their bitterness. On the other hand, they're perfectly happy being fried, steamed, or microwaved.

Calendar	Energy	Nutritional advantages
	25 kcal per 100 g	Rich in vitamins and minerals. Although quite low in calories, eggplants can soak up alarming amounts of fat.

Eggplants harmonize superbly with garlic, onions, tomatoes, bell peppers and zucchini, giving us the much-vaunted ratatouille. They are also the ideal accompaniment for lamb and grilled fish, and combine happily with thyme, herbes de Provence, Parmesan cheese, and cèpes, whose pronounced taste is close enough to be mistaken for that of the purple fruit.

Eggplants, simplicity itself

Broiled eggplants with lemon and parsley

> 2 eggplants > olive oil > 4 tablespoons lemon juice > flat-leaf parsley > cooking salt <

• Wash the eggplants but do not peel, then slice into ½-inch rounds. • Arrange the slices on the broiler rack with the broiler pan below; sprinkle with cooking salt, then drizzle with olive oil. • Broil the eggplants for 5 minutes on each side. • Transfer the slices to the serving plate. Sprinkle with lemon juice and top with plenty of chopped parsley. • Serve while still hot, or warm or cold, according to preference.

✛ Eggplants can be griddled or cooked on the barbecue. Serve this dish on its own as an appetizer, or with some cold meat. Broiled eggplant makes a good base for all sorts of salads, such as mozzarella, tomato, garlic, and basil salad, or feta, arugula, tomato, and fresh almond salad.

Penne alla Norma

> 2 eggplants > 4 tablespoons olive oil > 2 garlic cloves > 1 small can peeled tomatoes > 14 oz penne pasta > freshly grated Parmesan cheese > salt <

• Cut the eggplants into cubes using a really sharp kitchen knife. • Heat the olive oil in a pan and soften the garlic cloves and the eggplant cubes. • Once the eggplant is quite soft, add the drained tomatoes. • Cook for 15 minutes over a low heat, allowing the tomatoes to thicken and reduce. • Cook the pasta in plenty of boiling salted water until tender. • Drain well and tip into the sauce. • Mix and serve topped with the grated Parmesan cheese.

✛ Serve, as the Italians do, with a salad of arugula leaves dressed with lemon juice and extra-virgin olive oil.

Eggplant caviar

> 4 eggplants > 1 garlic clove > 1–2 tablespoons olive oil > salt <

• Peel the eggplants and cut into small cubes. • Crush the garlic in a garlic press. • Microwave the eggplants for 12 minutes in a lidded container with 1–2 tablespoons of water and a little salt. • Blend to a smooth paste, adding the crushed garlic and the olive oil.

✛ This recipe couldn't be simpler, thanks to the microwave. You could also impart a slightly smoky flavor by slicing the unpeeled eggplants in half and cooking them in a hot oven, then scooping out their flesh with a spoon before blending with the garlic and olive oil.

Eggplants with anchovies

> 4 fine thick-skinned eggplants > 32 small anchovies in oil <

• Preheat the oven to 350°F. • Halve the eggplants lengthwise. • With a sharp knife, cut 4 x ¼-inch gashes in each half and insert an anchovy in each of the cuts. • Arrange the eggplants in a baking dish and bake in the preheated oven for 20 minutes. • There's no need to salt this dish, as the anchovies are already salty enough.

✛ Prepared in a flash, this side dish goes well with all kinds of broiled meat.

Stuffed eggplants

> 4 fine thick-skinned eggplants > olive oil >
1 small bunch parsley > 1 slice from a rustic loaf,
crusts removed > 2 tablespoons milk > 1 egg >
14 oz ricotta cheese > 5-oz piece of smoked bacon,
cut into matchstick-sized pieces > grated Parmesan
cheese (optional) > salt and freshly ground black
pepper <

• Preheat the oven to 250°F. • Halve the eggplants
lengthwise. • Place on a baking tray, brush with olive
oil, season with salt and pepper, and bake in the
preheated oven for 45 minutes. • Chop the parsley.
• Crumble the bread and soak in the milk and beaten
egg. • Mix the ricotta, bacon, chopped parsley, and
soaked breadcrumbs in a bowl. • When the eggplants
are soft, remove them from the oven and scoop out the
flesh, taking care not to tear the skins. • Mix the
cooked flesh with the stuffing in the bowl, then use this
mixture to fill the eggplant shells. • Raise the oven
temperature to 350°F and bake for a further 20
minutes.

You can jazz up the stuffed eggplants by
sprinkling them with grated Parmesan cheese
just before baking.

Eggplant tart with preserved
lemon and tapenade

> 7 oz bread dough or 1 ready-made pizza base >
2 eggplants > ½ preserved lemon > 3 tablespoons all-
purpose flour > olive oil for cooking > 2 tablespoons
tapenade > 5 sprigs basil, finely chopped > salt and
freshly ground black pepper <

• Preheat the oven to 400°F. • Roll out the dough and
place it, or the pizza base, on a baking tray lined with
waxed paper; prick with a fork and bake in the

preheated oven for 15 minutes. • Rinse the eggplants
but do not peel; cut into large cubes. • Cut the
preserved lemon into small dice. • Roll the eggplant
cubes in the flour and pan-fry for 7–8 minutes in olive
oil. • Salt sparingly, season with pepper, and add the
diced lemon. • Remove the tart base from the oven. •
Spread with tapenade while still warm, then top with the
eggplant mixture. • Serve at once, sprinkled with the
chopped basil

Serve this tart cut into little squares as an
appetizer, or as a main course accompanied
by a green salad.

Eggplants with tomatoes
and mushrooms

> 1 garlic clove > 2 onions > 4 mushrooms >
4 eggplants > 8 tomatoes > 5 tablespoons olive oil
> a few thyme flowers > salt and freshly ground black
pepper <

• Preheat the oven to 275°F. • Peel and thinly slice
the garlic and onions. • Wipe and finely slice the
mushrooms. • Wash but do not peel the eggplants
and tomatoes, and cut them into ¼-inch slices. • Heat
2 tablespoons of the olive oil in a pan and fry the garlic,
onions, and mushrooms until the mushrooms have
rendered their moisture, then spread this mixture over
the base of an ovenproof baking dish. • Arrange
alternating slices of eggplant and tomato on top of the
mushroom mixture. • Dust with thyme flowers, season
with salt and pepper and drizzle with the remaining
3 tablespoons olive oil. • Bake in the preheated oven
for 1 hour.

Serve as an accompaniment to grilled fish or
meat. Eggplants and mushrooms are a match
made in heaven.

SUMMER VEGETABLES > eggplants

A fixture on market stalls all year round, cucumbers are nonetheless most appreciated at the height of summer for their refreshing crunch. This doyen of vegetables (it's one of the oldest kitchen-garden plants) is thus one of the most popular ones. Most often prepared raw, but sometimes cooked like zucchini, cucumbers improve on acquaintance. Their close cousins, pickling cucumbers, are prepared in various ways, but always as a condiment. Grown outdoors in the field, they're only available in the fine weather, for about three months, but modern methods of cultivation in plastic tunnels have extended this period.

Cucumbers and pickling cucumbers, a user's guide

American slicing cucumber 'Northern pickling', 'Conquest', 'Little Leaf' pickling cucumbers

American slicing cucumber: 'Jazzer' is probably the earliest slicer and has an average fruit length of 8 inches. 'Olympian' and 'Marketmore' are popular varieties with a crispy, fresh flavor. Some varieties have been developed in the "burpless" range.

Pickling cucumbers: People who want to pickle their own usually grow their own. 'Northern Pickling' was developed in Maine and is a high-yielding variety for the Northern states. 'Conquest' which develops good fruits from mini through to large. 'Little Leaf' was developed by the University of Arkansas and will cheerfully climb a trellis. The little leaves provide easier visibility of the fruits.

> **Choosing for quality**
Choose a really firm cucumber, with taut skin and no bruises.
Ideal size: The average size (between 14–20 oz) is ideal as it doesn't have too many seeds; no need to scoop out the seeds!!
Bad sign: If the cucumber is soft or shriveled at either end, choose another one.

> **Storage**
The charm of this vegetable is in its crunch; don't keep it waiting for too long, or it will go soft. Store for no more than 2 days in the vegetable compartment of the refrigerator.

> **Preparation**
To peel or not to peel? Small and medium-sized cucumbers have a thin skin that can be left on. Larger examples need to be peeled with a vegetable peeler.
Salt and drain, or seed? It's the seeds that upset sensitive stomachs, so it pays to seed cucumbers. Sprinkling coarse salt on slices of cucumber, rinsing them and patting them dry removes any bitterness, likewise a problem for certain people. Even if some varieties no longer suffer from bitterness, salting cucumbers also gets rid of excess water, and it's useful to avoid diluting the seasoning of a dish if it has to sit a while before being eaten.

Calendar

Energy
10 kcal per 100 g (98% water).

Nutritional advantages
Cucumber is known for its remineralizing virtues, its high betacarotene and vitamin B and E content. It also contains calcium, potassium and phosphorus. The pickling cucumber or dill pickle is similar in constitution to its cousin, although it is not, as was once thought, a "baby cucumber."

The cucumber is one of the oldest kitchen-garden plants, cultivated in Burma and India for more than 7,000 years. The king of summer salads, it marries deliciously with tomato, mint, tarragon, and all spices that harmonize with its distinctive flavor. Dill pickles are a condiment of which some people need their daily "fix."

Cucumbers and pickling cucumbers, simplicity itself

-20

"Carpaccio" of cucumber with red onion, soy sauce, and sesame

> 1 cucumber > 1 red onion > sesame seeds > 2 tablespoons soy sauce > 2 tablespoons sesame oil > 2 tablespoons balsamic vinegar > 1 teaspoon honey <

• Finely slice the cucumber. • Peel the onion and cut into small dice. • Toast the sesame seeds in a dry skillet. • Arrange overlapping slices of cucumber on each plate. • Add the diced onion, soy sauce, sesame oil, balsamic vinegar and honey. • Sprinkle with toasted sesame seeds.

+ A delightfully refreshing Japanese-style appetizer.

Cucumber "sushi"

> 2 cucumbers > sticky rice (special sushi or risotto rice) > salmon caviar or slices of smoked salmon <

• Peel the cucumbers and cut them into 1³/₄-inch sections with very stable bases. • Gently hollow out the cucumber sections with a small spoon, making sure you leave a base. • Cook the sticky rice. • Cut strips of smoked salmon, if using, and roll into pinwheel shapes as you would anchovy fillets. • Fill the inside of the cucumber cylinders with a little cooled rice and arrange a salmon pinwheel or a blob of salmon caviar on top.

+ Serve these "sushi" with little bowls of soy sauce for dipping. They are very trendy, and easier to make than the real thing.

Cucumber salad and goat's cheese with a curry dressing

> 1 cucumber > 1 fresh goat's cheese, or a slice from a "log" > 2 tarragon sprigs > 3 tablespoons white-wine vinegar > 1 tablespoon curry powder > 1 teaspoon pastis > 6 tablespoons olive oil <

• Peel the cucumber and cut it into thick rounds; arrange them in a salad bowl. • Cut the goat's cheese into thin slices. • Finely chop the tarragon leaves. • Prepare a vinaigrette by mixing together the vinegar, curry powder, pastis, and olive oil. • Pour the vinaigrette over the cucumber slices and leave to marinate in a cool place for 15 minutes. • Add the sliced goat's cheese and chopped tarragon leaves.

+ The goat's cheese can readily be replaced by a ewe's milk cheese in the summer (the best season for both these cheeses), or by fresh squares of demi-sel.

Cucumber sorbet

> 2 cucumbers > ¹/₂ cup orange juice > Tabasco > Worcestershire sauce <

• Peel the cucumbers and cut into chunks. • Blend until smooth, then transfer the purée to a bowl. • Add the orange juice, a few drops of Tabasco and a dash of Worcestershire sauce. • Churn in an ice-cream maker, or place in a rigid container in the freezer, breaking up the ice crystals with a fork every 15 minutes, until completely frozen.

+ Serve in little shot glasses with a cherry tomato split almost in half perched astride the lip of the glass, and a few cilantro leaves.

Did you know?

Cucumbers can be raised in an unheated green-house in the summer, they just need firm staking and string lines to cling to. Some varieties can be grown outdoors in a warm, sheltered spot, or in a grow bag if you only have a balcony or patio.

Hot tip

Cucumber with dip, cut into sticks and dunked in low-fat fromage blanc, or low-fat cream cheese, spiced with cumin or curry powder— a guilt-free pleasure!

Sautéed cucumber
with fresh salmon

> 1 cucumber > 3 salmon steaks > 8 dill sprigs >
olive oil for cooking > 3 tablespoons white wine >
6 tablespoons crème fraîche, thick yogurt or sour
cream <

• Rinse the cucumber and cut into sticks. • Cut the
salmon steaks into $\frac{1}{2}$-inch dice. • Finely chop the dill. •
Heat a little olive oil in a skillet and sauté the cucumber
sticks over a high heat. • Add the salmon cubes and
mix well. • As soon as the salmon cubes have taken on
a bit of color on each side (but are still raw in the
center), add the white wine, crème fraîche, and chopped
dill. Mix everything together and serve immediately.

✚ Make this recipe in a high-sided skillet or a wok,
so you can stir-fry all the ingredients and, most
importantly, not overcook the salmon. The salmon can
be replaced by cubed chicken.

Tzatziki

> 1 cucumber > coarse salt (if needed) > 1 garlic
clove > 2 sprigs fresh mint > 4 tablespoons lemon juice
> 4 pots (total about 10 oz) thick Greek yogurt > salt
and freshly ground black pepper <

• Peel the cucumber and grate it on the coarse side
of a box grater. • If you are not eating the tzatziki
straight away, sprinkle some coarse salt on the
cucumber and drain in a colander; then rinse the
cucumber and dry on paper towels before adding the
seasoning. • Transfer the grated cucumber to a deep
plate. • Crush the garlic in a garlic press. • Finely chop
the mint leaves. • Add the garlic, lemon juice, yogurt,
and mint to the grated cucumber. • Mix everything
together well, season with salt and pepper, and chill
in the refrigerator.

✚ Serve the tzatziki chilled with toasted pitta bread
or breadsticks for dipping.

Homemade pickles

> 2 lb fresh pickling cucumbers > coarse salt >
5 oz small white onions > 2 small sprigs thyme
> 2 bay leaves, crumbled > 5 cloves > 5 tarragon
leaves > 5 whole peppercorns > 10 coriander seeds
> 8 cups white vinegar <

• Wash and dry the cucumbers. • Cover the base of
an earthenware vessel with coarse salt. • Place the
cucumbers on top, then cover with more coarse salt.
• Let the cucumbers stand for 24 hours to release as
much of their water as possible. • Scald five glass
preserving jars to sterilize and prepare five equal piles
made up of the following ingredients: white onions,
thyme, bay leaf, cloves, tarragon, peppercorns, and
coriander seeds. • Rinse and dry the cucumbers. •
Divide them up between the jars and add the pickling
ingredients. • Fill each jar with white vinegar to cover. •
Seal hermetically and leave the jars undisturbed in a
dark place for 1 month.

✚ Pickling allows you to enjoy your cucumbers
beyond the summer months when they are in
season. Avoid spearing your them with a metal fork,
since vinegar and steel don't go well together; use
wooden tongs instead.

Members of the squash family (their name is Italian for "little squash'), zucchini are the essential summer vegetable. Sometimes reckoned to be a bit insipid, most of this vegetable's flavor—vaguely reminiscent of mushrooms or hazelnuts— is concentrated in the skin. The same goes for its vitamins—one more reason to save time by not peeling it. Zucchinis are prepared cooked—which distinctly highlights their sweet flavor—as well as raw.

Zucchini,
a user's guide

Long, green zucchini (Defender, El Greco...)
Round zucchini
Gold Rush zucchini
Mini zucchini and its flower
Marrow

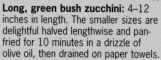

Long, green bush zucchini: 4–12 inches in length. The smaller sizes are delightful halved lengthwise and pan-fried for 10 minutes in a drizzle of olive oil, then drained on paper towels.

Round zucchini: Ideal for stuffing, pick ones no larger than a tennis ball.

Gold Rush zucchini: This variety is a bright yellow, earlier and fruitier-tasting. The vibrant color makes any dish attractive, especially mixed with its green siblings and red bell peppers.

Mini zucchini: A short blast in the microwave (with a tablespoon of water) is all that's needed. Add a teaspoon of crème fraîche or thick yogurt and a pinch of sea salt.

Zucchini flower: Stuffed, it's a true delicacy. A bit time-consuming to prepare, you may wish to leave this one to professional chefs. As a fritter or simply pan-fried, it's a "must"!

Marrow: Seed before eating; cooked rather than raw. Marrows are a very British vegetable, but are easily grown. Just leave one or two zucchini on your plant to carry on growing. Feed and water copiously and be prepared to relocate—they can grow quite big!

> **Choosing for quality**
Choose shiny, scratch-free specimens. The stalk should be hard to break: your guarantee of prime freshness. Out of season, zucchini are often imported and not necessarily raised in open fields, and are hence less flavorful.

Ideal size: For long varieties, choose ones measuring 6–8 inches/3 1/2–8 oz apiece. For the smaller varieties, choose ones that are 6 inches maximum in length—they'll be that much younger and beautifully sweet.

Bad sign: A dry or withered stalk means that the vegetable is less than spanking fresh.

Storage
> Zucchini dislike heat and scratches; keep them in the fridge. They spoil and soften quickly, though—don't keep them hanging around for too long.

Preparation
Washing Rinse, but never peel them.
>

Calendar	Energy	Nutritional advantages
	30 kcal per 100 g	The zucchini is high in vitamins A, C and E.

Zucchini harmonize brilliantly with fresh herbs, as well as with cumin, curry, and all oriental spice mixtures, which they absorb well. Together with eggplants, tomatoes, peppers, onions, and garlic, zucchini are the sixth essential ingredient in the much-loved ratatouille. Each plant has large male and female flowers fertilized by pollen-gathering insects. The baby zucchini springs from the base of the female flower

Zucchini, simplicity itself

Grated raw zucchini salad

> 4 small zucchini > 1 garlic clove >
3–4 sprigs of fresh herbs (cilantro, chives, or mint) > 3 tablespoons crème fraîche or thick yogurt > salt <

• Rinse and top and tail the zucchini. • Grate them on a carrot grater (or the side of a mandoline that produces thin slices). • Salt lightly, and if necessary, let them shed a little water in a colander for 15 minutes, then gently squeeze them in paper towels. • Crush the garlic in a garlic press. • Finely chop the herbs to obtain one tablespoon • Place the grated zucchini in a bowl and add the crème fraîche, chopped herbs and garlic. • Stir to combine.

+ There's no need to salt and drain the vegetables if you are serving the salad straight away; this step simply makes sure that the seasoning isn't "drowned" if the dish is left to wait a while. You can also dress the grated zucchini with a classic vinaigrette, or one flavored with walnut or hazelnut oil.

Zucchini tagliatelle

> 4 small zucchini > 2 tablespoons extra virgin olive oil (or use pesto, or $\frac{1}{2}$ teaspoon cumin powder) > 2 tablespoons crème fraîche or thick low fat yogurt <

• Rinse and top and tail the zucchini. • Cut into strips with a vegetable peeler or mandoline. • Cook this 'tagliatelle' for 1–2 minutes in a steamer or in the top basket of a pressure cooker, or microwave for 5 minutes (following maker's instructions). • Transfer the zucchini to a plate, season with your choice of flavorings and add the crème fraîche. • Gently mix everything to combine.

+ This is equally good served with meat or fish. Preparing the zucchini in this very simple manner gently highlights their nutty flavor.

Pan-fried round zucchini

> 6 round zucchini > 2 tablespoons olive oil > $\frac{1}{2}$ clove garlic > 1 parsley sprig > sea salt <

• Rinse and top and tail the zucchini, then cut them in half, horizontally. • Fry the zucchini halves for 5 minutes on each side in the olive oil until softened. • Drain well on paper towels. • Meanwhile, finely chop the garlic and parsley. • Season with sea salt at the last minute to preserve the crunch, and sprinkle with the chopped garlic and parsley. • Serve immediately.

+ No need to seed these 100-percent-edible, round zucchini. Once September has arrived, accentuate the hazelnut flavor of this quintessential summer vegetable by chopping a few of the first fresh walnuts of the season and sprinkling them over the top.

Zucchini and goat's cheese tart Tatin

> 5 zucchini > 10 chive stalks > 4 oz goat's cheese > olive oil for cooking > 1 garlic clove, crushed > 4 tablespoons raisins > 1 batch plain pastry (*see recipe p. 146*) > freshly ground black pepper <

• Preheat the oven to 350ºF. • Rinse the zucchini and cut into rounds. • Finely chop the chives. • Crumble the goat's cheese. • Sauté the zucchini in a pan with some olive oil and the garlic clove. • Add the chopped chives and tip everything into a

Cadge a plant or two from a gardening friend and grow your own. They also are happy in grow bags and you'll have a delicious fresh vegetable right to hand.

gratin dish, arranging the first zucchini rounds flat on the base of the dish, then overlapping them. • Add the raisins and crumbled cheese, season with pepper and cover with the pastry, tucking it well into the inside of the dish to seal in the vegetables. • Cut a cross in the center and bake in the preheated oven for 40 minutes. • Turn out upside-down onto a plate before serving.

✚ Serve as an appetizer, or as main course accompanied by a green salad. The interplay of sweet and savory is quite delightful.

Minted zucchini terrine

> 1¾ lb zucchini > 3 onions > splash of olive oil for cooking > 1 cup (tapped down) breadcrumbs, from day-old bread > ½ cup milk > ½ bunch fresh mint > 4 eggs > butter (optional) > 1 pinch grated nutmeg > salt and freshly ground black pepper <

• Preheat the oven to 350°F. • Rinse the zucchini and cut into rounds. • Finely slice the onions. • Heat the olive oil in a large skillet and sauté the zucchini and onions for 10 minutes, until softened. • Now crush the contents of the pan with a fork, or blend. Set aside. • Soak the breadcrumbs in milk, then drain well. • Finely chop the mint. • Separate the eggs, lightly beat the yolks and pour into the vegetable mixture, add the soaked breadcrumbs and chopped mint, season with salt and pepper, and add the grated nutmeg. • Lastly, beat the egg whites until stiff and gently fold into the mixture. • Butter a terrine dish (or line with waxed paper). • Tip the contents of the skillet into the terrine and bake in a water bath (place in a roasting tin filled with hot water half way up the terrine) in the preheated oven for 35 minutes. • When cooked, allow to cool in the oven with the door ajar.

✚ Serve chilled with a tomato sauce (*see recipe p. 59*), or with a spoonful of well-seasoned fromage blanc.

Zucchini tian

> 2 lb zucchini > butter (optional) > 2 garlic cloves > 8 parsley sprigs > 1 cup milk > 1 cup freshly grated Gruyère cheese > salt <

• Preheat the oven to 350°F. • Wash the zucchini and cut into rounds. • Blanch for 5 minutes in boiling salted water. •· Let drain for as long as possible (at least 1 hour). • If you don't have the time to do this, sauté them in butter for 10 minutes, keeping a sharp eye on them. • Tip the zucchini into a tian (or gratin dish). • Chop the garlic and finely chop the parsley; combine. • Pour the milk into a bowl and add the garlic and parsley mixture along with half the grated Gruyère cheese. Mix to combine. • Pour this mixture into the earthenware dish and top with the remaining Gruyère. Bake in the preheated oven for 30 minutes.

✚ You can season this tian with a pinch of ground cumin or curry powder, or with another oriental spice mixture—the zucchini will love it, though the children might not.

Iced zucchini soup

> 6 zucchini > 2 chicken bouillon cubes, dissolved in 4 cups boiling water (or homemade chicken bouillon) > 4 ice cubes > 4 tablespoons light cream > 1 teaspoon *ras-al-hanout* (Moroccan mixed spice) <

• Rinse the zucchini and cut into thick rounds. • Cook in the chicken bouillon until tender. • Allow to cool. • Blend, and add the ice cubes, cream and *ras-al-hanout*. • Transfer to a soup tureen.

✚ Serve garnished with shavings of Parmesan cheese, coarsely chopped cilantro and a drizzle of hazelnut oil to top it all off.

Zucchini, simplicity itself

Zucchini chips and zucchini-flower fritters

> 4 zucchini, with flower still attached > 7/8 cup all-purpose flour > 1 egg > 6 ice cubes > oil for deep-frying > sea salt, salt and freshly ground black pepper <

• Separate the flowers from the zucchini. • Wash the zucchini and cut them into chips. • Prepare a tempura batter by blending the flour, egg, ice cubes, and a pinch of salt and pepper. • Heat oil in a high-sided pan until a cube of bread browns in 30 seconds • Dip the zucchini chips and flowers in the tempura batter, shake off the excess and deep-fry until golden brown. •·Drain the fritters on paper towels before serving immediately with sea salt.

✚ Serve plain, or with a tomato coulis or tartare sauce. The same recipe may be used to make eggplant "chips."

Plain zucchini flowers sautéed in olive oil

> zucchini with flowers still attached > olive oil for cooking > sea salt and freshly ground black pepper <

• Make several slices in the zucchini and fan them out without detaching them from their flowers. • Sauté in olive oil. • Season with sea salt and pepper and serve immediately.

✚ A highly elegant accompaniment for meat or grilled fish.

Round zucchini filled with cod brandade

> 8 round zucchini > 10 oz cod brandade (see below) > fine breadcrumbs > freshly grated Comté (or Gruyère) cheese > olive oil > salt <

• Preheat the oven to 350°F. • Rinse the zucchini. Remove the stems and even out their bases by cutting as needed, so that the zucchini are nice and stable. • Cook for 5 minutes in boiling salted water.·• Cut off a lid from each zucchini and carefully hollow out the body. • Stuff the zucchini with the cod brandade and dust with the breadcrumbs and grated Comté (or Gruyère). •

Arrange the zucchini in a gratin dish and top with their lids. • Salt the lids and pour a drizzle of olive oil over everything. •·Bake in the preheated oven for 30 minutes.

✚ Brandade is salt cod pounded to a purée with olive oil, garlic, and milk and is a speciality of Provence. It is available in cans from specialist grocers. Serve this dish as a starter, or as a main course accompanied by a mixed green salad (see p. 68).

Marrow au gratin

> 1 marrow > 4 onions > tomatoes > olive oil for cooking > grated Gruyère cheese <

• Preheat the oven to 350°F. • Peel and seed the marrow, then cut it into small chunks. • Peel the onions and slice into rounds. • Rinse the tomatoes and slice into rounds. • Heat the olive oil in a skillet and soften the marrow and onions (you'll probably have to do this in several batches). • Transfer the mixture to a gratin dish and top with a layer of tomatoes. • Sprinkle with grated Gruyère and bake in the preheated oven for 15 minutes, until the top is golden brown.

✚ Serve with barbecued sausages or hamburgers, and you've got summer on a plate!

Pasta with zucchini and capers

> 6 zucchini > 2 garlic cloves > 4 tablespoons parsley > olive oil for cooking > 14 oz pasta > 3 oz piece Parmesan cheese > 2 tablespoons capers > salt <

• Rinse and grate the zucchini. • Crush the garlic. • Chop the parsley. • Sauté the grated zucchini in a little olive oil with the crushed garlic in a deep skillet for 15 minutes. • Meanwhile, cook the pasta in plenty of boiling salted water until tender. • Shave the Parmesan with a vegetable peeler. • Drain the pasta and tip into the skillet with the zucchini; add the shaved Parmesan, chopped parsley and capers. • Mix together everything well and serve.

✚ A Sicilian recipe that will whisk you from your kitchen to the slopes of Mount Etna.

Appropriately enough, the French bean was the first vegetable consumed by the French in its frozen form (it freezes very successfully) as well as tinned. Only 20 percent of green beans are destined for the fresh market. The fact is that French beans have long suffered from a flaw that nowadays exists only in our minds: their strings. With the new varieties, strings are a thing of the past, and the extra-fine filet or stringless beans can be eaten whole without fear.

Green beans, a user's guide

Stringless green French bean
Stringless yellow French bean
Wax bean
French filet beans
Flat pole beans

Stringless green French bean:
This is the most common variety. It is stringless like the filet, but bigger and fleshier, being machine-picked at a later stage.

Stringless yellow French bean:
Prized for its tenderness. Choose really fleshy specimens. It is usually hand-picked, and hence far more expensive than its cousin, the stringless green bean.

Filet French bean: This bean is the most costly variety. Thinner and more longline than the stringless green, as it's picked at a less mature stage, and hence by hand. It is therefore more expensive, but boasts an incomparable flavor.

Flat pole bean: A shape and texture that lend themselves to being cut into an attractive diamond shape.

> **Choosing for quality**
Choose really firm, velvety, unbruised beans. The bean should snap cleanly when bent, and a bead of sap should form at the base of the break.
Ideal size: The same for all, so that they all cook in the same time.
Bad sign: Avoid soft, dull-colored beans.

> **Storage**
Store French beans for as short a time as possible. Succulent on the day they are picked, they soon soften, and the vitamin content fades along with the quality! If you must store them, wrap them in a plastic bag and stow them in the vegetable drawer of your refrigerator for no longer than 2–3 days. Above all, don't trim them, as this hastens the aging process. Otherwise, store them cooked.

> **Preparation**
Washing A simple rinse will do the trick.
Trimming or destalking Hold the stalk between your thumb and index finger and snap it off cleanly, or use kitchen shears.
Cooking This is the crux of the matter, since French beans can go from undercooked to overcooked in a flash
Rule No. 1 Cook the beans in a large volume of boiling water (4 quarts per 2 lb) so that the water comes back to a boil quickly once the beans have been added; don't use an aluminum pot (which discolors the beans) or a pressure cooker (it would be impossible to control the degree of doneness).
Rule No. 2 Add salt to the water only once it comes to a boil. Tip in the beans right after you've added the salt, leave uncovered and keep the flame high. Depending on variety and size, time from 7 minutes to 15 minutes maximum. To tell when to stop the cooking, lift out a bean with a slotted spoon and check.
Rule No. 3 To serve cold in salads, drain the beans and plunge immediately into a bowl of ice water to arrest the cooking process and preserve their color and flavor. If you haven't the time to prepare a bowl of iced water, rinse them under cold running water for 2 minutes.
Rule No. 4 To serve hot, drain beans thoroughly in a colander, or by heating them in a dry pan while gently turning them: when no more steam rises, you can season and serve.

Calendar

Energy
24 kcal per 100 g

Nutritional advantages
Rich in protein, fiber, vitamins (including B) and minerals (potassium, among others), French beans are a figure-friendly vegetable.

Green beans are a breeze to prepare: no need for fiddly recipes to make the most of their flavor. Butter or cream, parsley, cilantro or mint, or a lovely warm vinaigrette, and you're in vegetable heaven! The only tricky bit is cooking them perfectly (see recipe p. 44).

Green beans, simplicity itself

French beans in vinaigrette dressing

> 2 lb French beans > 1 tablespoon balsamic vinegar > 3 tablespoons extra virgin olive oil > salt and freshly ground black pepper <

• Trim the green beans and cook them in boiling salted water. • Prepare a vinaigrette with the balsamic vinegar and olive oil. • Season with salt and pepper. • Pour the vinaigrette over the beans while they are still warm.

+ Try another, equally delicious vinaigrette made from sherry vinegar and hazelnut oil. Serve as is, or as a "designer" salad, adding chopped red onion, parsley or basil, pine nuts, strips of smoked duck breast and Parmesan shavings.

Green beans Italian-style

> 2 onions > 3 tomatoes > 2 lb French beans > olive oil for cooking > 1 thyme sprig > salt and freshly ground black pepper <

• Peel the onions and slice into rounds. • Peel and quarter the tomatoes. • Rinse and trim the green beans. • Heat some olive oil in a pan and sauté the onions and tomatoes. • When the tomatoes have softened and cooked down, add the green beans. • Season with salt and pepper, add the thyme sprig and cover. • Cook for 10–15 minutes over a low heat, stirring occasionally.

+ These beans are the ideal accompaniment for barbecued meat, or serve them with a veal saltimbocca to continue the Italian theme.

French beans with anchovy butter

> 2 lb French beans > 4 anchovies in oil > 1 shallot > 2/3 cup white wine > 4 oz chilled butter > coarse salt <

• Trim the beans and cook them in boiling salted water. • Transfer at once to a bowl of iced water, then drain. • Place the beans on a serving plate. • Whizz the anchovies and shallot in the blender. • Pour this mixture into a pan, add the white wine, and, removing the pan from the heat, add the butter a little at a time. • Whisk lightly until the mixture thickens slightly. • Pour the anchovy butter over the French beans.

+ Serve these beans, warmed by their dressing, as an appetizer, or as an accompaniment for tuna or grilled beef: the anchovy will partner either of them beautifully.

Hot buttery French beans

> 2 lb French beans > butter > salt <

• Trim the French beans and cook them in boiling salted water. • Drain the beans and drive off any remaining water by heating them for a few minutes in a dry pan. • Add a knob of butter and serve immediately.

+ Ring the changes by softening a shallot in butter, adding the cooked beans, and sautéing them together just before serving. Use one shallot per 1 lb of French beans.

Cold flat pole beans in a creamy curry dressing

> 1½ lb flat pole beans > 8 parsley sprigs
> 1 teaspoon curry powder > 4 tablespoons thick
crème fraîche or yogurt > cooking and sea salt <

• Rinse and trim the flat pole beans. • Cut into 1-inch
lengths (diamond shapes if you like) and cook for
20 minutes in 4 cups boiling salted water. • Meanwhile,
chop the parsley. • Allow beans to cool, then transfer to
a serving dish. • Just before serving, toss with the curry
powder, crème fraîche, and chopped parsley. • Adjust
seasoning with sea salt.

✛ With its lovely orange-and-green colors, this
creamy dressing is a delight for the eyes as
well as the tastebuds.

Big mixed salad of tuna with French beans and radishes

> 1 lb each of green beans and yellow beans
> 10–12 pink radishes > 4 tomatoes > 4 hard-cooked
eggs, shelled > tapenade > 2 x 6-oz cans finest quality
tuna in oil > 1 tablespoon capers > 4 anchovy fillets
> salt and freshly ground black pepper <

• Trim the beans and cook in plenty of boiling salted
water. • Transfer at once to a bowl of iced water,
then drain. • Rinse the radishes and tomatoes and cut
into rounds. • Halve the eggs lengthwise and spread
with tapenade. • Drain the tuna. • Transfer the beans
to a salad bowl and add the radishes, tomatoes, tuna,
anchovies and capers. Season. • Crown this festival
of colors with the tapenade-topped hard-cooked eggs.

✛ Enjoy this salad at the height of summer, when
you're back from the beach, for example. A quick
one-dish meal for appetites sharpened by the sea air.

French-bean parcels with smoked bacon

> 2 lb French beans > 8 thin slices of smoked sreaky
bacon > salt <

• Trim the beans and cook them in plenty of boiling
salted water. • Cook the bacon in a skillet without any
additional fat. • While still hot, wrap the bacon around
little bundles of the beans and secure the parcels with
small toothpicks. • Arrange the parcels in a heatproof
dish and reheat under a moderate broiler. • Serve
immediately.

✛ Serve these bean parcels with meat or fish;
their smoky flavor goes well with both.

First cultivated more than 4,000 years ago on the high plateaus of Mexico, "Indian corn" made its conquest of Europe thanks to Christopher Columbus. Nowadays, cultivated corn kernels are most commonly processed into cornflakes or popcorn, or ground into polenta; the whole kernels, however, are most often frozen or canned. When fresh, and picked immediately on ripening, corncobs are a delicious, tender, crunchy vegetable which can be boiled or broiled whole, while the baby corn cobs have also become popular. Canned, corn loses none of its nutrients.

Corn,
a user's guide

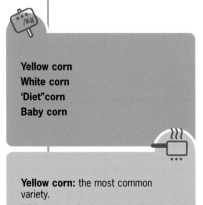

Yellow corn
White corn
'Diet"corn
Baby corn

Yellow corn: the most common variety.

White corn: Popular principally across the southern United States.

"Diet"corn: Has a higher water content than its cousins, and is hence lower-calorie

Baby corn: This mini variety is delightful in salads and stir-fries.

> **Choosing for quality**
Choose really firm ears with tight, still-green husks. The kernels should ooze sap if nicked.
Ideal size: There is no one ideal size.
Bad sign: Dry husks! Nothing for it but to use the ears as a decorative table centerpiece.

> **Storage**
Fresh corn must be picked while still immature, before the sugar in the kernels turns to starch. Like all fresh products, use quickly.

> **Preparation**
To shuck or not to shuck? Once freed from their husks, the ears can be steamed or cooked in boiling salted water for about 15 minutes, or baked for 1 hour, turning regularly. Alternatively, barbecue or grill the ears with their husks on.

Calendar

Energy
15 kcal per 100 g
(93–95% water).

Nutritional advantages
Rich in vitamins, mineral salts, fiber and protein. Low in fat. Canned corn has a similar nutritional content to fresh.

Fresh corn is an early delicacy. Cooked in its husk and served as is, or with its plump kernels cut off the ear, this grain-cum-vegetable harmonizes beautifully with poultry and all sorts of roast meats.

Corn, simplicity itself

Barbecued ears

> 4 corn ears > butter <

• Soak the corn ears still in their husks, pulled tightly closed around the ear, for an hour. • Barbecue the corn ears in their husks for 15 minutes, turning them on all sides. • When the corn ears are done and the husks peeled back (but not removed), guests put a knob of butter on their corn or pour over melted butter and eat it using the husk as a handle.

✛ Corn is most definitely not just for chickens! Serve these barbecued ears with grilled meat or poultry.

Cream of corn soup

> 4 corn ears > 2 chicken bouillon cubes, dissolved in 4 cups boiling water (or homemade chicken bouillon) > 4–5 pinches chilli powder > salt and pepper <

• Discard the husks and steam or cook the corn ears in boiling salted water for 15 minutes. • Remove the cooked kernels from the ears with a fork. • Add the kernels to the chicken bouillon and simmer for 5 minutes. • Blend in an electric blender until smooth, and adjust the seasoning to taste. • Spice up with the few pinches of chilli powder.

✛ Garnish with strips of smoked duck breast or grated cheese for a full meal with an unusual touch. You could also prepare this cream soup with a large can of corn.

Hot tip

Baby corn, just lightly sautéed in butter, or added to a stir-fry vegetable medley.

Corn and French bean fritters

> 8 oz canned corn (or 3 large corn ears) > 4 oz French beans > 2 scallions > 1 egg > scant ¾ cup cornstarch > 2 tablespoons chopped cilantro > light oil for frying > coarse salt (if necessary) <

• Drain the corn, or if using fresh ears, steam or cook in boiling salted water and remove the kernels from the ears with a fork. • Trim the French beans and cook for 15 minutes (see p. 44); cut into ¼-inch pieces. • Finely slice the scallions, including the green stems. • Mix the corn kernels and beans in a bowl. • Add the egg, cornstarch, cilantro and scallions. • Combine all the ingredients with your hands, then form the mixture into little balls. • Flatten these into fritters and fry in a little oil in a very hot pan. • Drain thoroughly on paper towels before serving.

✛ Serve with roast chicken for a lunch that is sure to go down well with the younger generation.

Corn 'blinis'

> 3 eggs > 6 tablespoons all-purpose flour > 1 cup warm milk > light oil for frying > 1 large can corn, drained > salt <

• Prepare a crêpe batter by mixing together the eggs, flour, and warm milk (heating the milk eliminates any need to rest the batter). • Season sparingly with salt. • Heat a little oil in a blini pan (or small skillet or griddle) and fry little crêpes, spooning a few corn kernels into the center of each blini.

Serve these blinis as an accompaniment for meat or as an appetizer, rolling them around a slice of ham and a salad leaf.

Corn, roast chicken, and sun-dried tomato salad

> 2 boneless cooked chicken breasts > 16 cherry tomatoes > 8 sun-dried tomatoes > 1 large can corn > vinaigrette (see recipe p. 145) > fresh herbs (chives, chervil or parsley) <

• Cut the chicken breasts into pieces. • Halve the cherry tomatoes. • Cut the sun-dried tomatoes into small dice. • In a salad bowl, combine the drained corn with the chicken and both types of tomatoes. • Prepare a vinaigrette in another bowl; pour it over the salad ingredients and toss well to mix. • Add some finely chopped herbs if desired to garnish.

Sun-dried tomatoes are readily available in supermarkets in various forms.

Mixed corn salad with rice and tuna

> ½ cup long-grain rice > 1 large can corn > 2 x 6 oz cans tuna steak > 2 tomatoes > ½ green bell pepper > ½ cucumber > 1–2 scallions > vinaigrette (see recipe p. 145) <

• Cook the rice in boiling salted water for 10 minutes or until tender; drain and rinse under cold running water. • Drain again thoroughly and tip into a large salad bowl. • Drain and flake the tuna, drain the corn and add to the rice. • Dice the tomatoes and bell pepper, slice the cucumber into thin rounds, and finely slice the scallions including the green stem into rounds. • Add

all the vegetables to the salad bowl. • Prepare a vinaigrette (see p. 145) and pour it over the salad; toss everything well to combine.

Rice tends to soak up a lot of vinaigrette, so it's better to stress the corn rather than the rice, reversing the proportions of the traditional rice salad.

Mexican rice

> 1 onion > 1 carrot > oil for cooking > 1 cup long-grain rice > ½ cup corn kernels > ¾ cup peas > 2 tablespoons tomato paste > 1 chicken bouillon cube, dissolved in a cupful of boiling water <

• Peel and finely slice the onion. • Peel the carrot and slice into rounds. • Heat a little oil in a pan and sauté the onion until golden; add the rice. • When all the rice grains are thoroughly coated, add the carrot rounds, corn kernels, peas, tomato paste, and chicken bouillon. • Add just enough water to cover and cook over a low heat covered with a tight-fitting lid until all the liquid has been absorbed, about 10 minutes. (If the rice is a bit underdone, add a little more water and cook for a few minutes longer). • Turn out onto a serving dish and serve immediately.

For a more authentically Mexican, spicy version, sauté a finely sliced chile along with the onions, taking care to remove all the seeds from the chile (unless, of course, you like your food really spicy!).

Bell peppers and chiles belong to the same family, specimens of which Columbus brought back from his first and subsequent voyages to the Americas. The sweet pepper is a very demanding plant as far as temperature is concerned, and is mainly greenhouse-grown. High-quality, reasonably priced bell peppers are available year round. Red peppers are actually green peppers, picked two weeks later on. Yellow and orange peppers are different varieties. As for chile peppers, they embrace a whole range of flavors, with varying intensities of heat.

Sweet bell peppers and chiles, a user's guide

Green bell pepper
Red bell pepper
Yellow bell pepper
Orange bell pepper
Small red piquillo pepper
Baby bell pepper
Long pepper

Green bell pepper: The most common type, with a more pronounced and bitter taste than the others.

Red bell pepper: Sweeter and more fruity than the green.

Yellow bell pepper: Sweeter than green.

Orange bell pepper: Sweeter than the green.

Small red piquillo pepper: This is the one that's stuffed and bottled (mainly in Spain). Although the smallest of the family, it's anything but short on flavor. So thin-skinned that it doesn't require peeling.

Baby bells: To gradually accustom children to appreciating the adult version of the vegetable.

Chile pepper: There's a great variety of these, but beware the jalapeño and habanero, they are very hot.

Long pepper: To spice up a dish, or use in an omelet.

> **Choosing for quality**
Choose firm, shiny, unblemished peppers and chiles with intact stalks.
Ideal size: Hardly an issue, it's up to you.
Bad sign: Dry or withered stalks mean that the peppers or chiles are less than spanking fresh.

> **Storage**
Thanks to their glossy skin, bell peppers can easily keep 4-5 days in the refrigerator after purchase.
Strung into scarlet curtains on the fronts of houses—a frequent sight in Mediterranean countries—chiles can be dried outdoors for using much further down the line.

> **Preparation**
Washing Rinse peppers and chiles under running water.
Seeds and ribs Aside from their unpleasant mouth feel, the seeds of peppers, but especially of chiles, should be removed, because it's there that the capsaicin—the chemical compound responsible for their heat—is concentrated. This will make it easier for you to control the heat of the finished dish. Remove the ribs (inner veins or membranes) of the peppers. Wear protective gloves and wash your hands thoroughly after handling chiles: do not put your hands anywhere near your eyes, it can be very painful!
Peeling Peppers and chiles can be eaten with or without their skins, but are more easily digested without them. Nothing is simpler than skinning a pepper. There are two ways to go about it: simply peel the raw pepper with a vegetable peeler, or cook it first. If going for the second option, bake the whole peppers in a hot oven until their skins swell and blister. Then seal them in a plastic bag or plastic wrap until they cool, and finally, remove their skins (they virtually peel themselves), then their ribs and seeds under a trickle of running water (this avoids your having to remove the seeds one by one).

Calendar

j j a s
As well as the rest
of the year

Energy
20 kcal per 100 g

Nutritional advantages
Bell peppers are exceptionally rich in vitamin C (antioxidant, combats stress and fatigue) and in pro-vitamin A (the growth vitamin).

First off, peppers go really well with each other! Mixing green, red, and yellow peppers gives agreeable contrasts of both color and taste. They also harmonize well with cumin, garlic, onions, eggplants, and tomatoes, to name a few. Bell peppers are an essential ingredient of an authentic gazpacho or ratatouille. As for chiles, they crank up the heat in spice mixtures.

Sweet bell peppers and chiles, simplicity itself

-20° Trio of sautéed bell peppers

> 2 each green, red and yellow bell peppers > 1 small long chile pepper > 1 onion > 2 garlic cloves > olive oil for cooking > salt and freshly ground black pepper <

• Rinse the bell peppers and remove the seeds and ribs and cut into strips. • Wash the chile pepper, remove the seeds and ribs, and slice finely. • Peel the onion and cut into rounds. • Crush the garlic in a garlic press. • Heat some olive oil in a skillet and sauté the vegetables until they begin to catch. • Add about ½ cup water and let the vegetables caramelize gently until the liquid is absorbed. • Season with salt and pepper.

+ Serve hot with chunks of tuna, or strips of boneless chicken breast pan-fried in olive oil and deglazed with soy sauce, or as an accompaniment to pasta or fried eggs.

Piperade

> 2 onions > 2 garlic cloves > 2 green bell peppers > 4 tomatoes > chili powder > 4 eggs > 4 fine slices ham, preferably Bayonne > olive oil for cooking > salt and freshly ground black pepper <

• Peel and finely slice the onion and garlic. • Rinse and seed the bell peppers and cut them into strips. • Peel and seed the tomatoes. • Heat some olive oil in a large skillet and sauté the garlic and onion until golden. • Add the strips of pepper and the tomatoes. • Season with salt, pepper and chili powder to taste, and let the mixture caramelize for 30 minutes. • Break the eggs over the vegetables and stir over a low flame as for scrambled eggs. • Meanwhile, fry the slices of ham over a low flame, covered, and serve with the piperade.

 A great Basque Country classic, which makes a perfect lunch or light supper.

Red pepper sorbet

> 4 red bell peppers > 1 garlic clove > 4 tablespoons lemon juice > 4 basil leaves, torn into pieces > Tabasco > salt and freshly ground black pepper <

• Rinse the peppers and steam them. • Seed and peel the cooked peppers. • Crush the garlic clove. • Blend the pepper flesh with the crushed garlic, lemon juice, basil, a pinch of salt and pepper, and a few drops of Tabasco. •·Add sufficient water to give the consistency of fruit juice. • Churn in an ice-cream maker or place in a rigid container in the freezer, breaking up the ice crystals with a fork at regular intervals, until the sorbet is of the right consistency.

+ Serve at the height of summer between courses as a palate cleanser, topped with a pinch of oregano.

Chilled cream of yellow pepper soup

> 6 yellow peppers > 2 garlic cloves > 2 potatoes > 2 leeks (white part only) > butter for cooking > 1 chicken bouillon cube, dissolved in 2 cups boiling water (or homemade chicken bouillon) > 1 cup light cream > feta cheese to garnish (optional) <

• Rinse and seed the peppers, then cut into strips. • Crush the garlic cloves in a garlic press. • Peel the potatoes and cut into rounds. • Slice the leeks. • Melt some butter in a sauté pan and soften all the vegetables. • Add the chicken bouillon and cook for

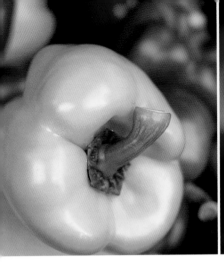

20 minutes. • Allow to cool, then refrigerate. • Finally whizz in an electric blender until smooth, adding the light cream.

 This creamy pepper soup can be served in prechilled cups with a little feta cheese crumbled on top.

Pasta with red peppers, tomatoes, and arugula

> 2 red bell peppers > 1 red onion > 2 large tomatoes > 2 generous handfuls arugula leaves > olive oil for cooking > 2 tablespoons balsamic vinegar > 2 tablespoons sugar > 14 oz pasta > Parmesan cheese, for garnish (optional) >salt and freshly ground black pepper <

• Rinse and seed the peppers and cut them into strips. • Peel the onion and cut into rounds. • Peel and quarter the tomatoes. • Pick through the arugula; rinse and dry in a salad spinner. • Heat some olive oil in a large skillet and sauté the peppers and onion. • When the peppers begin to soften, add the balsamic vinegar and sugar, then caramelize over a low heat for 10 minutes. • Add the quartered tomatoes. • Meanwhile, cook the pasta in plenty of boiling salted water until tender. • Pour the finished sauce into a large serving dish. • Drain the pasta, tip into the serving dish and add the arugula. • Toss all the ingredients together well and season to taste.

 Add a few shavings of Parmesan, or the spicier pecorino, just before serving.

Sweet pepper terrine with cumin and garlic

> 3 each red and green bell peppers > 3 garlic cloves > 2 teaspoons ground cumin > olive oil > salt and freshly ground black pepper <

• Rinse the peppers. • Place them on a baking sheet in a hot oven until their skins blister and swell. • Remove from the oven, seal the peppers in a plastic bag or place in plastic wrap until cool. They should now peel easily. • Remove the ribs, and seeds under a trickle of running water. • Slice the flesh of the peppers into strips. • Crush the garlic in a garlic press. • Arrange the strips of pepper in a terrine mold or on a large serving plate. • Season with salt and pepper and sprinkle with the crushed garlic and cumin. • Drizzle over some olive oil to cover and leave in a cool place for 12 hours before serving.

Serve at the table straight from the dish; or pile on slices of toasted bread, or as a tapas dish to accompany an aperitif.

Tomatoes, which are actually a fruit, belong to a huge family numbering no less than 10,000 species. Available all year round, they are nonetheless at their most flavorful at the height of summer. Native to Central and South America, the tomato was known to the Aztecs by the name of tomatl. What would we do with them?

Tomatoes, a user's guide

Plum tomato
Vine tomato
Cherry tomato
Beef tomato
Super beefsteak tomato
Oval plum tomato
Green tomato
Yellow tomato
Orange tomato
Black tomato

Oval plum tomato: Thick-fleshed and not too juicy (so no need to seed), this tomato won't waterlog your pizza base or tart.

Vine tomato: Ideal raw in salads.

Cherry tomato: Queen of the cocktail hour, this tomato can be cut in two and skewered on a toothpick with a mini mozzarella ball or an olive.

Super beefsteak tomato: Slice off a lid and replace. Stuffed or served Provençal-style; barbecued or griddled.

Green tomato: Use to make delicious fried green tomatoes (remember the *Whistle Stop Café* film?). It is a tomato variety in its own right and not merely an unripened one.

Yellow tomato and Orange tomato: Sweeter than red tomatoes, they make a nice surprise when included along with them in a salad.

Black tomato: Almost no tartness, and hence very much in favor with children, plain or in a salad.

> ## Choosing for quality
Tomatoes should have smooth, shiny skin, and be firm to the touch and well-coloured. Their skins should be a vivid red, a uniform green for the green varieties, or an unequivocal bright yellow. Their stalks should also be firm and a fine dark-green in color.

Ideal size: No larger than a clementine for ordinary globe tomatoes. Bigger than this, and tomatoes contain a lot of seeds. Of course, this does not apply to the beef and super beefsteak varieties.

Bad sign: Soft tomatoes will have been fingered by too many prospective buyers; they'll only be fit for a coulis. Nonuniform color means the fruit is not ripe. If too pale, the fruit may not be ripe and, therefore downright tasteless.

> ## Storage
Store at room temperature in a basket or fruit bowl, like other fruits. Avoid storing tomatoes in the refrigerator, which will alter their taste and destroy their nutrients. Once perfectly ripe, do not store them for more than 3 days.

> ## Preparation
Washing Don't wash tomatoes until you are ready to use them, and make sure you remove their stalks after, not before rinsing, or they will become waterlogged.

Peeling For or against? There are two schools of thought: those in favor of removing the skin, whether the tomatoes are used raw or cooked, and those who insist on leaving it on. The first-case scenario is a bit tedious, but highlights the silkiness of the sweet flesh; on the other hand, a proportion of the vitamins lodged just under the skin is lost. In the second-case scenario, maximum benefit is derived from this vegetable's potential, if you disregard the little bits of skin in cooked dishes, which can be discreetly pushed to the edge of one's plate. However, some people just cannot digest the skins, so peeling is then a must.

How to peel them Plunge the tomato in boiling water for about 30 seconds then drain. With a sharp knife, cut a cross at the stem end and the skin will easily slide off. This action is known as "blanching".

Seeding Cut the tomato into quarters and scrape out the seeds with a small spoon.

Calendar	Energy	Nutritional advantages
a m j j a s	15 kcal per 100 g (94% water)	Rich in vitamin C and carotene (stimulant), lycopene (anti free-radical) and potassium.

Raw or cooked, tomatoes harmonize magnificently with peppers, zucchini, and eggplant, as well as fish, ham, and olives...a vegetable for all seasons, so to speak.

Tomatoes, simplicity itself

Tomato salad

> Vine tomatoes > extra-virgin olive oil > balsamic vinegar > fresh herbs stripped from their stalks (basil, flat-leaf parsley, chervil or cilantro) > sea salt and freshly ground black pepper <

• Rinse and quarter the tomatoes and place them in a salad bowl. • Pour over some olive oil and balsamic vinegar to taste. • Finely chop some fresh herbs and sprinkle on top. • Add the sea salt and bring the pepper mill to the table.

✚ If you have 10 extra minutes to spare, peel the tomatoes for an even better salad.

Pan bagnat or club sandwich

> $^1/_4$ baguette (or 1 small, round crusty roll) > fromage frais > vine tomatoes > cucumber > a few salad leaves > hard-cooked eggs > cooked meat (sliced chicken, ham) or tuna > sea salt and freshly ground black pepper <

• Slice open the baguette or roll and spread with fromage frais. • Rinse and slice the tomatoes and cucumber. • Wash and dry the salad leaves. • Slice the eggs. • Arrange the vegetables, meat and sliced egg in the baguette or roll and season with sea salt and pepper.

✚ This sandwich makes a complete meal which will delight the kids.

Stuffed tomatoes

> Large beefsteak tomatoes > about 3 oz stuffing per tomato (*for stuffing suggestions see below*) > pine nuts > salt <

• Choose tomatoes of the same size so that they all cook in the same time. • Preheat the oven to 350°F. • Rinse the tomatoes, cut off a lid and gently hollow out the insides with a small spoon. • Reserve the flesh. • Salt the tomatoes, turn them upside down and leave on some paper towels for 15 minutes to remove excess moisture before stuffing them (see below for suggestions). • Add a few pine nuts to the stuffing and fill the tomatoes with the mixture. • Arrange the tomatoes in a gratin dish, placing their reserved flesh on the bottom of the dish to prevent them from sticking. • Bake in the preheated oven for 35 minutes. • Serve hot.

✚ Make a stuffing by cooking up some rice and adding whatever takes your fancy: tuna, mushrooms, chopped walnuts, herbs, cooked minced meat, etc.

Tomato crisp

> 2 lb plum tomatoes > 2 onions > olive oil for cooking > 4 oz butter > $1^1/_3$ cups all-purpose flour > $1^1/_4$ cups freshly grated Parmesan cheese > 4 tablespoons pine nuts > pepper > 1 tablespoon sugar > 1 tablespoon fresh thyme leaves <

• Preheat the oven to 250°F. • Rinse and quarter the tomatoes. • Peel the onions and slice into rounds. • Heat some olive oil in a skillet and sauté the tomatoes and onions until the onions are golden. • In a large bowl, with your fingers combine the softened butter, flour, Parmesan cheese and pine nuts into a crumb mixture. • Season with pepper. • Oil a gratin dish and spread the tomato-onion mixture over the base. • Sprinkle with sugar and thyme. • Drizzle over a trickle of olive oil and bake in the preheated oven for 1 hour (the

Did you know?

Tomatoes play a key role in the Cretan diet—the benchmark for healthy, balanced eating.

Hot tip

The tomato slicer—a utensil that cuts tomatoes into uniform rounds in a flash!

tomatoes should be dry). • Remove the dish from the oven and raise the temperature to 400°F. • Scatter the crumb mixture evenly over the tomatoes, add a final drizzle of olive oil and bake for an additional 25 minutes until golden brown.

+ Serve the tomato crisp warm, accompanied by a dollop of really cold thick crème fraîche, or a mixture of soft goat's cheese and light cream. This recipe can also be made with zucchini instead of tomatoes.

Tomato sauce

> 8 medium-sized, well-ripened globe tomatoes. > 1 large onion > olive oil for cooking > 3 garlic cloves > 1 bouquet garni (parsley, thyme, bay leaf) > salt <

• Peel the tomatoes (see Preparation p. 56), then halve, seed and crush them. • Peel and chop the onion;. chop the garlic. • Heat some olive oil in a skillet and sweat the onion in the hot oil. • Add the crushed tomatoes, chopped garlic, and bouquet garni to the pan. • Season with salt, and cook for 45 minutes over a low heat, letting the sauce caramelize.

+ To make a succulent base for a tomato tart, spread the finished sauce on some prebaked puff pastry. Top with anchovy fillets, a little mozzarella and a few olives, and brown under the grill for a few minutes before serving. To ring the changes with this sauce, you could add $\frac{1}{2}$ teaspoon of freshly grated ginger at the end of the cooking time, which will lend an additional fresh note.

For homemade bolognaise sauce, add 1 cup ground beef and a carrot sliced into rounds at the same time as the onions. Ladle onto pasta, sprinkle with fresh Parmesan and serve at once. The kids will love it!

Al fresco tomato soup

$2\frac{1}{2}$ lb ripe vine tomatoes > $\frac{3}{4}$ cup bottled tomato juice > 1 tablespoon tomato paste > $\frac{1}{2}$ garlic clove > 2 tablespoons ketchup > $\frac{1}{2}$ teaspoon ground fennel (or celery salt) > $\frac{1}{2}$ teaspoon Worcestershire sauce > 2 tablespoons lemon juice > basil or tarragon leaves <

• Place all the ingredients except for the fresh herbs in a food processor and blend until smooth. • Strain the soup through a sieve and refrigerate for at least 2 hours. • Serve chilled, sprinkled with chopped basil or tarragon.

+ For a spicier taste, rinse 10 canned anchovies and marinate overnight in the soup before blending. Serve with slices of baguette rubbed with garlic or spread with tapenade, or a guacamole-style avocado dip.

Beet is the root of a plant from the chard and spinach family. From May to December it can be found in supermarkets and market stalls, raw and often with its leaves on. Beet is also sold cooked, however, and is available all year round boiled or baked in its skin. Generally served cooked and cold, beet is also to be found in some delicious hot dishes, and can be prepared raw as well. There are three main types of beet: the garden beet, which we are dealing with here; the fodder beet, used to feed cattle; and the sugar beet, which is refined into sugar.

Beets,
a user's guide

Long beet
Round, raw beet with its leaves
Round, boiled beet
**Round, baked beet
  (wrinkled skin)**

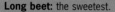

Long beet: the sweetest.

Round, raw beet with its leaves: Even its leaves can be eaten (prepared like Swiss chard). The root is eaten raw, after peeling and slicing, like grated carrot, but more strongly seasoned. It can also be cooked for 2 hours in its skin, then peeled. It's important to cook whole beet in its skin so that it doesn't lose its juice or color in the cooking water.

Round, boiled beet: Found most often in this form, it can be recognized by its smooth skin, which must be removed before it is eaten.

Round, baked beet: Less common, it can be identified by its wrinkled skin and delicious, smoky flavor.

> **Choosing for quality**
Cooked beet mustn't be scratched, much less moldy.
Ideal size: None
Bad sign: If the skin is damaged, choose another.

> **Storage**
Beet can easily be stored refrigerated for 3–4 days.

> **Preparation**
Peeling cooked beet This is the only thing you need do before eating it—although some vacuum-packed beet is already peeled.

Calendar	Energy	Nutritional advantages
	45 kcal per 100 g (the same as two lumps of sugar)	Rich in vitamins, fiber and calcium.

Ninety percent of the time beet is found on supermarket shelves in its cooked form. The recipes here therefore use mainly cooked beet. This ruby-colored vegetable can be served hot or cold in a number of variations, however, as a change from the perennial pickled beet.

Beets, simplicity itself

 ### Beet chips

> 1 cooked beet > oil for frying (if required) > salt <

• Preheat the oven to 225°F. • Peel the beet and cut into very thin slices. • Dry the sliced beet in the preheated oven for 1½ hours, or fry for 10 minutes in a deep-fryer, then drain on paper towels. • Salt as you would potato chips.

✛ Serve as an appetizer with drinks, or as a garnish—plant them stegosaurus-style in vegetable mash, (your children will know what I mean!).

Creamy beet soup

> 4 zucchini > 2 cooked beets > 1 cup freshly grated Gruyère cheese > 2 tablespoons light cream or crème fraîche, thick yogurt or sour cream > coarse salt <

• Rinse the zucchini and cut them into chunks. • Peel and coarsely chop the beets. • Cook the zucchini chunks for 10 minutes in boiling salted water. • Add the chopped beet and bring back to a boil. • Blend contents of pan until smooth. • Add the grated cheese and cream or yogurt and blend again.

✛ Serve with a few crushed hazelnuts sprinkled over the top, and a drizzle of hazelnut oil if desired.

Beet "carpaccio" with cilantro

> 2 cooked beets > ½ bunch cilantro > balsamic vinegar > olive oil > sea salt <

• Peel the beets and cut into thin slices using a mandoline or food processor. • Arrange the slices on the serving plate. • Finely chop the cilantro and scatter it over the beet carpaccio. • Season with the balsamic vinegar, olive oil and sea salt.

✛ You can vary this salad by dicing the beet (the flavor will be different) and seasoning the vinaigrette with cinnamon: you'll be agreeably surprised by the taste.

 ### Mashed beet

> 4 large potatoes > 2 cooked beets > 3 tablespoons light cream > 1 pinch grated nutmeg > salt and freshly ground black pepper <

• Peel the potatoes and cook them in boiling salted water as for a classic mash (*see recipe p. 118*). • Peel and quarter the beets. • Push the potatoes through a potato ricer and the beet pieces through a *mouli*; combine. • Add the cream and grated nutmeg, then season with salt and pepper. • Mix thoroughly before serving.

✛ Sprinkle finely chopped parsley over the mash before serving as a perfect accompaniment for game or roast meat, or with broiled sausages.

Pink salad of beet, chicory, apple, and walnut

> 3 small cooked beets > 2 heads chicory > 1 apple > 1 tablespoon grain mustard > 1 tablespoon sherry vinegar > 3 tablespoons olive oil > a few walnut kernels > salt and freshly ground black pepper <

• Peel and dice the beets. • Rinse the chicory and cut into thin rounds. • Peel the apple and cut into

Hot tip

Watch out for the "Chioggia" variety that has rings of white and red and looks very attractive on the plate.

thick slices, then cut the slices into two. • Make a vinaigrette with the mustard, vinegar, and oil. • Season to taste, add the walnuts, and toss everything together well.

+ You can replace the chicory with lamb's lettuce if wished.

Beet, cucumber, and watercress salad with horseradish

> 3 small cooked beets > $1/2$ cucumber > 1 red onion > 2 handfuls watercress > 2 tablespoons lemon juice > 2 tablespoons horseradish > 4 tablespoons heavy cream > salt and freshly ground black pepper <

• Peel the beets and cut into thin rounds. • Wash the cucumber and cut into thin slices. • Peel and finely dice the onion. • Pick through the watercress, wash and drain. • Place all the vegetables into a salad bowl. • Mix the lemon juice, horseradish and heavy cream in a bowl. • Season to taste and pour over the salad.

+ If you're not keen on horseradish, substitute a tablespoon of fine mustard.

Beet and goat's cheese salad

> 2 cooked beets > fresh chives > sherry vinegar > light vegetable oil > 1 goats' cheese log > salt and freshly ground black pepper <

• Peel and julienne the beets (cut into very thin match-stick-sized pieces). • Place in a salad bowl. • Finely chop the chives. • Prepare a classic vinaigrette dressing with the vinegar, oil, salt and pepper, then season the beet and add the chives. • Mix together well. • Just before serving, cut the cheese into rounds and place them on top of the beet salad without tossing.

+ Toss this salad at the very last minute or you'll end up with some very odd-looking pink goats' cheese.

Roasted beet

Roasting fresh beet is both easy and delicious. • Preheat the oven to 400°F. • Trim the roots and leafy tops to leave a flat base on which the beets will stand. • Place whole baby beets (or larger ones cut in half) on a large piece of foil, drizzle with olive oil, and season. • Wrap the foil into a parcel, place in an ovenproof dish and roast for 30–40 minutes. • The beets are ready when you can pierce them easily with the point of a knife. • Serve baby beets whole or sliced. Peel larger ones before serving.

+ Delicious mixed with cubes of goat's cheese in a salad.

Celery root (also known as celeriac) and celery are descended from the same wild plant, known as smallage (or wild celery). One developed the bottom of its stem and the top of its root to form a large tuberosity (celery root); the other has an essentially above-ground lifestyle (celery). Thus, unlike what is sometimes believed, one is not the root of the other. Both, however, share a very similar flavor and the same characteristic scent. Root or stem, celery is eaten raw or cooked, but each variety is prepared in its own particular way. Their basic difference lies in their textures

Celery and celery root, simplicity itself

Celery root (celeriac)
(Stalk) celery

Celery root: Just one variety exists—the same one first mentioned in Italy in the early 16th century.

Celery salt: Based on dried, powdered celery root, this is essential for mixing a Bloody Mary, and can also be used to season plain tomato juice.

Celery (stalk): A cousin of celery root, stalk celery is a wholly distinct variety. Some varieties are very white, others green. Much depends on the "earthing up."

> **Choosing for quality**
For celery root, choose a firm, heavy root. Celery should have firm stalks that snap easily.
Ideal size: Small celery roots are less likely to be hollow, but a fine big 2-lb specimen can also be very good.
Bad sign: A withered celery root covered with brown spots or which sounds hollow is a vegetable fit only for chicken feed!

> **Storage**
Celery root is a "keeper": It can be stored for weeks without a problem in the vegetable compartment of the fridge.
Stalk celery, however, spoils more quickly: store it wrapped in a damp cloth, for no longer than 4 days.

> **Preparation**
Peeling Celery root is peeled like a potato. If you must keep it waiting, squeeze lemon juice over it or place it in acidulated water, as its flesh quickly darkens on contact with the air.
Washing and stringing Celery needs a little rinse after the first row of outside stalks are removed. Remove any tough fibers from the ribs.
How to remove the fibers To remove the tough fibers from celery stalks, cut the base of the stem but not quite through, pull back and off and the fibers will come away in strings.

Calendar

Energy
44 kcal per 100 g (celery root);
20 kcal per 100 g (celery).

Nutritional advantages
Rich in cellulose (good for sluggish intestines), calcium, phosphorus and trace elements. They also contain sodium.

Celery root is one of the star ingredients in a pot-au-feu and other fall and winter stews, to which it adds a peerless aroma. Generally, it is used cooked like a potato, which it sometimes advantageously replaces (in a gratin dauphinois, for example). Celery is a delight in limited amounts—one stalk is enough—in all mixed vegetable soups, where it adds a delicate flavor. It can also be dipped in salt and a bit of fresh butter and munched raw, like a radish.

Celery and celery root, simplicity itself

Cream of celeriy root soup

> 1 celery root > 1 chicken bouillon cube, dissolved in 2 cups boiling water > ⅔ cup light cream or crème fraîche > salt and freshly ground black pepper (if required) <

• Peel the celery root and cut into large cubes. • Cook in a pan with the chicken bouillon until all the liquid has been absorbed. • Blend in an electric blender until smooth, then slacken the purée with the light cream. • Taste and adjust seasoning if necessary.

+ Lovers of spicy food can season this soup—already very flavorful—with ground cumin or turmeric if desired. Adding tumeric will give the soup a beautiful orange color. You could also mellow its flavor by boiling two potatoes along with the celery root.

Celery braised in bouillon

> 1 head of celery > 2 tablespoons butter > 2 tablespoons concentrated veal bouillon or 1 chicken bouillon cube > 2 sugar lumps or 1 teaspoon sugar <

• Prepare the head of celery by washing and cutting it into chunks and removing the strings. • Melt the butter in a pan and sauté the celery chunks until softened. • When the celery is golden, add 1¾ cups water, the veal bouillon or chicken bouillon cube and the sugar. • Cover and simmer for 30 minutes over a low heat until tender.

+ Serve as an accompaniment to white meat or poultry, for a delicate and subtle mixture of flavors.

Celery root remoulade

> ½ celery root > mayonnaise (see below) > 1 egg yolk > 2 tablespoons fine mustard > grapeseed oil > sea salt <

• Peel the celery root, then grate on the side of a box grater (like one that you'd use for carrots). • Blanch in boiling salted water for 5 seconds to preserve the whiteness and crunch. • Drain well and transfer to a salad bowl. • Allow to cool. • Prepare some mayonnaise (see recipe p. 147) using twice as much mustard as usual: mix the egg yolk, pinch of sea salt and mustard, and whisk in the grapeseed oil

+ Add some diced apple and/or 1 tablespoon curry powder to your celery root remoulade for a classic with a brand new twist that you won't ever grow tired of!

Brandade of smoked haddock with celery root

> ½ celery root > 1 large potato > 14 oz smoked haddock > 1 cup milk > 1 garlic clove > 1 thyme sprig > 1 bay leaf > chili powder > 1 tablespoon chopped parsley > 4 tablespoons breadcrumbs > salt <

• Peel the celery root and cut into chunks. • Peel the potato and cut into chunks of the same size. • Place the celery root and potato chunks in a pan, cover with salted water and cook for 15 minutes until tender. • Drain thoroughly and put the cooked vegetables through a potato ricer • Cut the smoked haddock into pieces. • Pour the milk and 1 cup water into a pan and add the whole garlic clove, thyme, bay leaf, chili powder, and a pinch of salt. • Add the pieces of haddock and bring everything

Hot tip

The heart of a celery stalk, served raw, the stalks filled with slightly salted cream cheese, like little boats, and sprinkled with chives, make a great appetizer.

to a boil. • Time for 2 minutes after it comes to a boil, then drain the fish, reserving the garlic clove. • Finely chop the garlic clove. • In a large bowl, coarsely crush the haddock with a fork. • Reheat the celery root purée slightly (in the microwave, for example) and add to the fish along with the chopped garlic, parsley, and olive oil. • Mix everything together well, check the seasoning and pour into a gratin dish. • Sprinkle with breadcrumbs and place under a preheated grill until the top is crusty and golden.

✚ Yves Camdebore, Chef at *La Régalade* in Paris, taught me this surprising brandade (*see p. 43*) recipe. A simple delight in which smoked haddock replaces the traditional salt cod, thereby eliminating the need to soak the fish.

 ## Cream of celery root soup with smoked bacon

> 1 celery root > $^2/_3$ cup light cream > 4-oz piece smoked bacon, cut into matchstick-sized pieces > coarse salt <

• Peel the celery root and cut into large chunks. • Cook in 2 cups of boiling salted water for about 40 minutes, until tender. • Blend the celery root in an electric blender until smooth and add the cream. • Reheat over a low heat. • Meanwhile, pan-fry the bacon and divide among shallow bowls. • Give the soup a final whizz in the blender or with a handheld electric blender just before serving to froth it up.

✚ For an elegant dinner-party touch, garnish the soup with one or two slices of bacon, oven-dried flat between two baking sheets.

Celery root and blue cheese quiche

> 1 small celery root > 1 cup crumbled blue cheese > 4 eggs > $^2/_3$ cup milk > $^2/_3$ cup crème fraîche or thick yogurt > 1 pinch grated nutmeg > 1 batch plain pastry (*see recipe p. 146*) > coarse salt > salt and freshly ground black pepper <

• Preheat the oven to 350°F. • Peel the celery root and shred it on the coarse side of a box grater. • Blanch the grated celery root for 5 minutes in boiling salted water. • Drain well. • In a large bowl, mash the cheese with a fork, then add the eggs, milk, and crème fraîche. • Season with salt and pepper and add the nutmeg. • Tip in the drained celery root. • Line a quiche pan with the pastry, pour in the celery root mixture and bake in the preheated oven for about 35 minutes.

✚ Served with a salad of corn salad (lamb's lettuce) with a few walnut kernels added for good measure, this is one of the joys of the season.

There are over 200,000 named species of fungi in the world. Of the 4,000 of these found in Europe, only one quarter are edible. The need for caution and the advisability of having your self-picked harvest checked by an expert can therefore not be stressed enough. Only several dozen varieties of mushrooms are truly prized for their gastronomic qualities. Wild or cultivated, all mushrooms are nutritional powerhouses

Mushrooms, a user's guide

Cèpe or porcini
Chanterelle or girolle
Morel
Cultivated mushroom
Truffle

Cèpes or porcini: raw or sautéed in oil, these call for simple treatment.

Chanterelle: These are the queens of the meadows and glades, along with their cousin, the horn of plenty. Delicate in texture, they need to be prepared with the greatest of care, and should never be washed in water like cèpes. They're at their finest with a shallot softened in oil. Garlic, on the other hand, tends to mask their delicate flavor.

Morel: The appearance of its pitted cap means that spring has arrived. **Take care—morels are toxic when raw.** Use them to flavor crème fraîche, for example. Rinse under a trickle of running water and drain in a salad shaker.

Cultivated mushroom: Large for stuffing, but range down in size to the button variety. Generally white or cream-colored, depending on the method of cultivation. If the cap is tightly closed, cut off just the base of the stalk and simply wipe the cap.

Truffle: Black, it's worth its weight in gold; white, in platinum—but what a delicacy! Bursting with flavor, a truffle must never be left in the open air. Truffles are at their best in December and January. Eat fresh, grated over the dish at the last moment.

> **Choosing for quality**
Choose mushrooms that are as young and fresh as possible. For cultivated mushrooms, the caps should still be attached to the stalks; for cèpes, the spongy pores should be as pale as possible.
Ideal size: Small mushrooms are firmer, but large ones have more flavor—so the choice is up to you.
Bad sign: A dried-out appearance or tunnels of worms running the length of the mushroom give away a harvest past its peak of freshness.

> **Storage**
As short a time as possible, and in any case in an airtight container in the refrigerator.

> **Preparation**
Washing or wiping clean Never wash mushrooms in lots of water, or dip them—even briefly—in vinegary water. Rinse them under a trickle of water, then brush them or wipe them with a damp cloth.
Scrape off or cut off the bottom of the stalk Remove the earthy film from the end of the stalks of cèpes and chanterelles with a small, pointy knife.
Getting rid of the worms in cèpes One trick consists in placing the mushrooms—stalks trimmed, caps wiped—spaced out on a plate. Cover with plastic wrap. Any worms will come out and stick to the film, which you simply throw away after an hour.
Getting rid of the worms in chanterelles Simply blanch the mushrooms for 1 minute in boiling salted water to drive out the worms. This operation has the additional advantage of setting the color of the mushroom.
Caution—fragile load! Mushrooms are delicate and break apart easily, so it is important to put them at the top of your shopping basket.

Calendar	Energy	Nutritional advantages
	From 15 to 45 kcal per 100 g (80-90% water).	Contain potassium, phosphorus, selenium, magnesium, iron, trace elements, protein, carbohydrate and B-group vitamins.

Mushrooms marry beautifully with all meat—white, red or game—but also team well with eggs, rice, and pasta, which they flavor to perfection.

Mushrooms, simplicity itself

"Carpaccio" of broiled cèpes

> 1 lb cèpes > ½ cup olive oil > 10 sprigs of mixed fresh herbs (parsley, cilantro, chervil, tarragon, basil) > sea salt > salt and freshly ground black pepper <

• Trim the bases of the stalks of the cèpes and wipe clean with a damp cloth. • Slice thinly and arrange them on a baking sheet. • Salt lightly, season with ground black pepper and drizzle with 3½ tablespoons of the olive oil. • Cook under a preheated broiler for 3 minutes. • Meanwhile, chop the herbs. • When the cèpes are done, arrange them on the plates in a rosette. • Sprinkle with sea salt and the chopped herbs, and drizzle with a last of the olive oil.

+ For a celebratory meal, accompany this carpaccio of cèpes with equally thin slices of foie gras.

Quick fricassee of exotic mushrooms

> 1½ lb mushrooms (use cèpes or chanterelles, or a mixture of both) > 3 shallots > 3 tablespoons goose fat, or butter > 5 sprigs flat-leaf parsley <

• Rinse the mushrooms, then chop them into large pieces. • Peel and thinly slice the shallots. • Heat the goose fat or butter in a skillet and sweat the shallots for 1 minute, then add the mushrooms. • Cook, stirring gently, until the mushrooms are golden all over. • Finely chop the parsley and sprinkle over the mushroom and shallot mixture. Serve immediately.

+ Pan-frying the mushrooms like this leaves them still firm inside, while preserving their flavor. You can also par-cook them in a dry pan over a medium heat until they release their natural juices. Discard the juices, then finish the mushrooms off in oil or butter over a high heat. They will have lost some of their firmness, but none of their flavor.

Braised cèpes with shallots and bacon

> 12 large cèpes > olive oil for cooking > 4 shallots > 4 thin slices smoked bacon > ¼ chicken bouillon cube, dissolved in ¾ cup boiling water > 1 thyme sprig > salt and freshly ground black pepper <

• Trim the bases of the stalks of the cèpes and wipe clean with a damp cloth. • Separate the stalks from the caps and slice the caps thinly. • Heat some olive oil in a skillet and caramelize the sliced mushroom caps on both sides. • Season with salt and pepper, and drain. • In the same pan, sear the stalks in a drop of olive oil. • Peel and quarter the shallots. • Arrange the mushroom stalks in a flameproof casserole with the shallots, bacon and the chicken bouillon add the thyme and season with salt. • Add the mushroom caps. • Cover and simmer for 15 minutes.

+ Cèpes prepared like this make a very simple but delicate-tasting appetizer or side dish.

Hot tip

The cultivated mushroom for stuffing, available year round, needs almost no preparation. Bite right into it raw, or cook with bold flavors. It's also the least calorific of the mushrooms, but filling owing to its fiber content. What more could you ask for?

Cream of mushroom soup

> 2 lb cultivated mushrooms > butter
for cooking > 1 chicken bouillon cube, dissolved in
4 cups boiling water > ¾ cup crème fraîche or thick
yogurt (use low-fat if you are watching the calories) <

• Rinse and finely slice the mushrooms. • Sweat in a
little butter in a pan. • Add the chicken bouillon and
cook gently, covered, for 30 minutes. • Add the crème
fraîche and blend until smooth in a liquidizer

+ Reserve one raw mushroom to slice thinly and
scatter on top of the soup bowls as a garnish.

Mushroom tart Tatin

> 1 lb mushrooms (cèpes, chanterelles, cultivated
mushrooms) > oil for cooking > 10 oz pearl onions
> 1 garlic clove > ¼ bunch flat-leaf parsley > 1 cup
diced smoked bacon > 1 sheet ready-made puff pastry
> salt and freshly ground black pepper <

• Preheat the oven to 425°F. • Rinse or wipe the
mushrooms and cut into thick slices. • Heat some oil in
a skillet and sauté until softened. • Drain and set aside.
• Finely slice the onions. • Peel and chop the garlic
clove. • Chop the parsley. • Sauté the onions, garlic,
and bacon in the same pan as the mushrooms. • Add
the chopped parsley. • Place the reserved mushrooms
on top and season. • Tip everything into a pie pan,
cover with the puff pastry, tucking it well into the the
dish to seal the contents, cut a cross in the center and
bake in the preheated oven for about 20 minutes. •
Turn out onto a plate and serve immediately.

+ Cooking the mushrooms under the pastry lid
in this way traps their wonderful aromas and
flavors for your dinner guests.

Mushroom risotto

> 1 onion > 1 garlic clove > 1 shallot >
8 oz mushrooms > 2 tablespoons goose fat, or butter
> 1¼ cups risotto rice > ¾ cup white wine > 1 chicken
bouillon cube, dissolved in 2½ cups boiling water >
butter for cooking > 1 tablespoon crème fraîche or
thick yogurt > ¾ cup freshly grated Parmesan cheese
> salt and freshly ground black pepper <

• Peel and chop the onion, garlic, and shallot. • Rinse
or wipe the mushrooms. Drain well. • Heat the goose
fat or butter in a sauté pan and cook the onion and
garlic until softened. • Tip in the rice. When the rice
has turned pearly white, pour in the wine and continue
cooking. Once it is absorbed, add the hot chicken
bouillon a ladleful at a time, stirring constantly.
Do not add the next ladleful until the previous one is
absorbed. • Meanwhile, heat a knob of butter in a skillet
and soften the mushrooms; add the chopped shallot,
and season with salt and pepper. • Combine the two
mixtures and add the crème fraîche and grated
Parmesan.

+ Use cèpes or cultivated mushrooms, depending
on the success of your harvest or availability at
the market.

Raw cèpes salad in vinaigrette

> 10 oz cèpes > 2 celery stalks > 8 cherry
tomatoes > 8 walnuts > 8 black pitted olives
> 1 cup diced bacon > light vegetable oil > walnut oil <

• Trim the bases of the stalks of the cèpes and wipe
clean with a damp cloth. • Slice the cèpes thinly. •
Cut the celery into small dice. • Quarter the cherry
tomatoes. • Shell the walnuts and crumble into large
pieces. • Slice the olives very finely. • Dry-fry the bacon

FALL VEGETABLES > mushrooms

Mushrooms, simplicity itself

in a non-stick pan. • Arrange the sliced cèpes on flat plates and sprinkle with the diced celery, tomato, walnut pieces, sliced olives, and bacon cubes. • Prepare a dressing with the two oils and drizzle it over the plates.

+ A very elegant appetizer, and simplicity itself to prepare. Make sure your mushrooms are spanking fresh and of top quality.

Mushroom custards

> 10 oz mushrooms (cèpes or cultivated)
> 1 shallot > 2 tablespoons butter > 2 eggs >
$\frac{1}{2}$ cup milk > $\frac{1}{2}$ cup light cream > 1 pinch nutmeg
> salt and freshly ground black pepper <

• Preheat the oven to 350°F. • Clean and coarsely chop the mushrooms. • Blanch for 1 minute in boiling salted water. • Drain, pressing well to remove any excess water. • Peel and thinly slice the shallot. • Sweat in a skillet with 1 tablespoon of the butter, then add the mushrooms. • Cook for 5–10 minutes, until all the natural juices have evaporated. • Whisk the eggs, milk and cream together in a bowl. • Season with salt, pepper, and nutmeg. • Tip the slightly cooled mushrooms into this mixture. • Butter some small muffin tins or ramekins and pour in the mixture. • Place the custards in a water bath (in a roasting tin filled with hot water to come half way up the ramekins) and bake in the preheated oven for 25 minutes.

+ Serve the custards turned out onto plates with a green salad.

Stuffed mushrooms

> 8 large mushrooms (cèpes or cultivated) >
10 oz pork loin > 2 slices boiled ham
> 2 onions > 2 garlic cloves > $\frac{1}{2}$ bunch flat-leaf parsley > 1 egg > 1 pinch grated nutmeg > fresh breadcrumbs > a knob of butter for cooking >
salt and freshly ground black pepper <

• Preheat the oven to 400°F. • Clean the mushrooms and cut off their stalks, reserving them for the stuffing. • Arrange the caps hollow side up in an oiled gratin dish. • Cut up the pork loin and ham, and chop finely in a food processor. • Chop the onions, garlic, parsley, and mushroom stalks. • Add these ingredients to the ground meat along with the egg and a pinch each of salt, pepper, and nutmeg. • Pulse to blend in the food processor one last time. • Stuff the mushroom caps with this mixture. • Sprinkle with breadcrumbs and dot each of the stuffed caps with a small knob of butter. • Bake in the preheated oven for about 20 minutes or until pork is thoroughly cooked.

+ Serve with a salad of young dandelion leaf, or curly endive in a very garlicky dressing.

Fish and mushroom parcels

> 6 large mushrooms (cèpes or cultivated) >
3 garlic cloves > 3 onions > olive oil for cooking
> the juice of 2 limes > 4 fillets of white fish >
salt and freshly ground black pepper > chopped herbs, to garnish <

• Preheat the oven to 350°F. • Clean the mushrooms. • Peel the garlic and crush in a garlic press. • Peel and finely slice the onions. • Heat some olive oil in a skillet and soften the mushrooms with the garlic and onions. • Season with salt and pepper and add the lime juice. • Cut out four sheets of aluminum foil to make individual wrappers for the fish. • Place a fish fillet in the center of each sheet, season with salt, and top with the mushroom mixture. • Seal the parcels, place on a baking sheet and bake in the preheated oven for about 20 minutes.

+ Once you've opened the parcels, sprinkle the fish with a little chopped parsley, tarragon or chives to garnish.

The family Cucurbitaceae embraces some 120 genera and 800 species, but those that particularly interest us here—commonly referred to as pumpkins or squashes—number a mere three: pumpkin, Hokkaido (or Japanese) squash and pattypan squash. The giant of the family is "the largest of all the fruits that creep on the earth," according to a 19th-century dictionary: it can weigh a good 20 lb on average, but the current world record is held by Dill's Atlantic Giant at 1,330 lb. When Halloween transforms pumpkins into chubby, leering faces lit up from the inside by a candle, it's the perfect occasion to harvest their flesh to use in some delicious recipes.

Pumpkin and squash, a user's guide

Pumpkin
Hokkaido squash
Pattypan squash

Pumpkin: Rouge Vif d'Étampes, flat and well ribbed, is the most common variety "Rouge vif" means "vivid red."

Hokkaido squash: Also known as Japanese Pumpkin or Kabucha, this "winter" squash is smaller than a pumpkin (it weighs between 4–8 lb. It has a characteristic chestnut flavor, and is thus in a class of its own. It is cooked like pumpkin, but does not need peeling.

Pattypan squash: White, green, orange, or variegated, this "summer" squash is generally only found on market stalls in September and October, during which months its pleasant nutty flavor works wonders. Like its cousins the pumpkin and Hokkaido squash, it can be cooked in many ways but its size makes it easy to hollow out and stuff. They range in size from the tiny "trouser button" to teacup.

> **Choosing for quality**
Choose specimens with fresh, firm, smooth flesh
Ideal size: There is no one best size, it depends on the variety.
Bad sign: Spots that are starting to go bad betray a specimen that has been in the cold or heat for too long.

> **Storage**
Whole, pumpkins and winter squashes can be kept for 3–6 months in a cool, dry place. Once they have been cut, store in plastic wrap and refrigerated for no longer than 3 days.

> **Preparation**
To peel or not to peel Peel pumpkins, but not Hokkaido or pattypan squashes; these should simply be seeded.
Removing the seeds and ribs Once you've cut it open, scoop out the seeds and membranes of the pumpkin with a tablespoon (and keep the seeds to plant the following winter).

Calendar	Energy	Nutritional advantages
	20 kcal per 100 g (95% water)	Rich in pro-vitamin A and carotene (which makes you look well).

Pumpkins and Hokkaido squashes are among the few vegetables that are eaten—always cooked—in both sweet and savory preparations. Although the rather bland taste of pumpkin needs spicing up, the original flavor of both Hokkaido and pattypan squashes requires more respect and less enhancement.

Pumpkin and squash, simplicity itself

Pumpkin gratin

> 1½ lb pumpkin > 1 teaspoon ground cumin, ginger, turmeric or coriander), or chopped tarragon (optional) > 1¼ cups freshly grated Gruyère (Comté, Beaufort or aged Parmesan) cheese > olive oil for cooking (if required) > coarse salt <

• Peel, seed and cube the pumpkin. • Microwave for 8 minutes in 1 tablespoon water with a little salt. • Alternatively, you can pressure-cook the pumpkin cubes for 10 minutes, steam them for 20 minutes, cook them in boiling salted water for 20 minutes, or stew in olive oil and ½ cup water in a covered skillet over a low heat for 25 minutes. • Drain well and add one of the spices or the tarragon, if using. • Tip everything into a gratin dish and sprinkle with grated cheese. • Grill until you have a nice, golden crust on top.

✚ Jazz up this gratin by sprinkling with crumbs made from a piece of stale gingerbread pulverized in your processor.

Halloween cream of pumpkin soup

> 2 lb pumpkin > 2 chicken bouillon cubes, dissolved in 4 cups boiling water > 1 teaspoon superfine sugar > 2 level tablespoons cornstarch > 1 cup light cream > grated nutmeg > chili powder (optional) > salt and freshly ground black pepper <

• Peel, seed and dice the pumpkin. • Place in a pan with the hot bouillon. • Bring back to a boil and cook for 20 minutes. • Add the sugar. • Blend well, return to the heat and add the cornstarch, dissolved in a little water, and the cream. • Check seasoning, adding salt, pepper, nutmeg, and chili powder to taste. • Briefly blend again before serving.

✚ If you are not averse to a richer soup, add 4 oz butter after the final blending. You can also replace the pumpkin with Hokkaido squash, in which case substitute mascarpone for the light cream.

Roast chicken with pumpkin

> 1 lb pumpkin > 1 medium-to large chicken > 1 garlic clove > extra virgin olive oil > salt and freshly ground black pepper <

• Preheat the oven to 425°F. • Peel and seed the pumpkin and chop into 2-inch cubes. • Season the inside of the chicken and stuff with the pumpkin cubes and whole garlic clove.• Drizzle olive oil over the chicken and season. • Place the chicken on its side in a roasting pan and cook in the preheated oven for 20 minutes. • Turn over onto its other side and roast for a further 20 minutes. • Place it flat for the final 5 minutes. Baste the chicken with its juices each time it is turned. • Make a final check by piercing the thickest part with a sharp skewer to make sure that the juices run clear. • Joint and carve the chicken and roughly mash the pumpkin, which will have absorbed the cooking juices, before serving.

✚ A complete one-dish meal, made in record time, that packs plenty of flavor.

Savory Hokkaido squash custards

> 1¼ lb Hokkaido or butternut squash > 4 tablespoons oil (olive, walnut, hazelnut or sesame) > 2 eggs > ½ cup milk > ½ cup light cream > butter for greasing > salt and freshly ground black pepper <

• Preheat the oven to 300°F. • Rinse, seed and dice the squash. • Microwave in a tablespoon of water with a little salt for 12 minutes. • Blend with your chosen oil, season with pepper and add the eggs, followed by the milk and cream. • Pour into buttered ramekins and bake in a water bath (in a roasting tin filled with hot water to come half way up the ramekins) in the preheated oven for 30 minutes.

 Serve with soft-cooked eggs and a side salad, or with broiled chicken escalopes or ham.

Pumpkin and orange caramel custards

> 1 lb pumpkin > 12 sugar lumps (or 2 oz superfine sugar) > 5 oz cornstarch > 3 cups milk > 1⅓ cups brown sugar > grated rind of 1 orange > juice of 3 oranges <

• Peel, seed and dice the pumpkin. • Microwave in a tablespoon water for 8 minutes. • Drain thoroughly, then blend until smooth. • Make a caramel with the sugar lumps and a little water, then pour it in the base of six ramekins. • Gradually mix the cornstarch into the cold milk. • Place in a pan and heat, stirring constantly. • As soon as it reaches a boil, tip in the brown sugar and orange zest and juice. • Cook, stirring, until the sugar has dissolved then add the puréed pumpkin, mix well and pour into the ramekins. • Allow to cool

 You can serve the custards in their ramekins, or unmold them first.

Pumpkin (or Hokkaido squash) tart with cinnamon

> 1¾ lb pumpkin (or Hokkaido or butternut squash) > 1 cup light cream > 3 eggs > scant ¾ cup raw sugar > 1 teaspoon ground cinnamon > 1 batch plain pastry (see recipe p. 146) <

• Preheat the oven to 350°F. • Peel, seed and dice the pumpkin or squash. • Microwave for 15 minutes. • Drain thoroughly, then blend with a handheld electric blender • Add the cream, eggs, sugar, and cinnamon. • Roll out and line a pie pan with the pastry and fill with the pumpkin mixture. • Bake in the preheated oven for 45 minutes.

 As soon as it's out of the oven, you can sprinkle the tart with ½ cup slivered almonds dry-fried in a pan for 30 seconds with the grated rind of ½ orange.

 ## Pattypan "nests" with cheese

> 4 pattypan squashes > 1 garlic clove > 2 shallots > 3 scallions > 10 oz fresh soft cheese > salt and freshly ground black pepper (or chili powder) <

• Rinse and steam the squashes for 10 minutes. • Crush the garlic, finely chop the shallots and scallions (use as much of the green stem as you like) and mix with the cheese. • Season with salt and pepper or chili powder. • Slice the top off each squash and fill with the cheese mixture, using a fork to combine the flesh and cheese. Level out the filling with the tops of the "nests."

 A fall version of Globe artichoke nests with cheese (see recipe p. 10).

Pattypans with garlic and parsley

> 16 mini pattypans > 1 bouquet garni > 1 garlic clove > 10 parsley sprigs > 1 knob butter > salt and pepper <

• Rinse and cook the pattypans for 10 minutes in boiling salted water with the bouquet garni. • Chop the garlic and parsley. • Pan-fry the cooked squashes for a few minutes in the butter with the garlic and parsley.

 Serve the pan-fried pattypans as an accompaniment to white meats.

FALL VEGETABLES > pumpkin and squash

With fennel, it's the bulb that's eaten. In the Middle Ages it was reputed to protect homes from evil spirits. Since the Renaissance it has been the favorite accompaniment to fish, which it remains to this day. As delicious cooked as it is raw, fennel brightens up fall and winter recipes. It belongs to the same family as dill, anise, star anise, caraway, coriander, cumin, and fenugreek. All these species share a common essence containing anethol, responsible for the characteristic aroma of anise, and a flavor that eclipses all others in the same dish.

Fennel,
a user's guide

Bulb fennel (Florence fennel)
Baby fennel
Herb fennel

Bulb fennel: There is only one variety of fennel, perfected during the Renaissance by the Tuscans from the wild plant that grows throughout the Mediterranean.

Mini fennel: A mild version of fennel suitable for children.

Herb fennel with umbellifers and seeds: If you have a fennel plant in your garden, make sure you save the dried stems. These can be used to make a delicious bed on which to cook fish. As for the seeds, they are used like cumin, again with fish, for example, or with Munster cheese.

> **Choosing for quality**
Choose firm bulbs of a fine white color with green stripes.
Ideal size: Small fennel bulbs are less fibrous than large ones, so choose the smallest ones available.
Bad sign: Brown spots and a mushy, stringy texture are the signs that the fennel was picked too long ago.

> **Storage**
Keep the fennel for no more than a few days in the vegetable compartment of your refrigerator, in an airtight container, as its aniseed aroma is likely to spread to other foods.

> **Preparation**
Washing Rinse the fennel and remove any outside leaves that are marked or spoiled. Cut off the base of the fennel and make a slight incision in the core, which can still be a bit tough even after cooking.

Calendar	Energy	Nutritional advantages
	20 kcal per 100 g	Rich in vitamins C and B, and in potassium, calcium and sodium, as well as fiber.

Crisp, sweet, and juicy, raw fennel is a tasty surprise in a number of mixed salads, not to mention the aromatic punch it packs: no need for fresh herbs alongside it! Cooked as a side dish, its distinctive taste still shines through.

Fennel, simplicity itself

Speedy fennel

> 4 fennel bulbs > crème fraîche (or butter, or 2 tablespoons lemon juice and some olive oil) > coarse salt <

• Rinse the fennel bulbs, cut out the cores, and quarter each bulb. • Cook for 6 minutes in a pressure cooker or for 20 minutes in boiling salted water or in a basket over steam. • The fennel is cooked when it can be easily pierced with the tip of a knife. • Arrange the fennel pieces on a serving plate and top with the crème fraîche (use low-fat if you are watching the calories), butter, or lemon juice and olive oil mixture, as desired.

➕ Maximum taste and healthiness, minimum calories. To ring the changes, you could blend the fennel and seasonings to a purée.

Braised fennel à la provençale

> 6 fennel bulbs > 2 garlic cloves > 4 tomatoes > ¾ cup pitted black olives > ¾ cup dry white wine > 10 fennel seeds (optional) > olive oil for cooking <

• Rinse the fennel bulbs, cut out the cores, and halve each bulb lengthwise. • Peel and chop the garlic. • Rinse and coarsely chop the tomatoes, peeling them if you wish. • Heat some olive oil in a sauté pan and soften the fennel, chopped garlic, tomatoes, and olives. • Add the white wine, ¾ cup water, and the fennel seeds (to accentuate the aniseed flavor, if required). • Cook, covered, over low heat for 1 hour.

➕ Serve hot or cold, as a vegetable accompaniment or on slices of toasted bread rubbed with garlic, as tapas.

Pasta with fennel, sardines, and raisins

> 2 fennel bulbs > 1 large onion > olive oil for cooking > 14 oz fresh sardine fillets > 2 anchovies in oil > ½ cup raisins > ½ cup pine nuts > 1 pinch saffron threads > 14 oz pasta > salt and freshly ground black pepper <

• Rinse the fennel bulbs and cut into small pieces. • Cook for 20 minutes in boiling salted water. • Drain, reserving the cooking water to add to the pasta cooking water. • Peel the onion and cut into small dice. • Heat some olive oil in a skillet and cook the onion until soft and golden. • Add the sardine and anchovy fillets and cook everything over a high heat for 5 minutes, breaking up the fish fillets with a spatula. • Add the drained fennel, raisins, pine nuts, and saffron. • Mix well, lower the heat and simmer on a low flame while the pasta is cooking. • Heat a large pan of water, adding the fennel cooking water. Add salt once it reaches a boil, and cook the pasta. • Once the pasta is al dente, drain, toss with the sauce, season with pepper and serve at once.

➕ You may wish to add a few tomatoes to this typically Sicilian recipe.

Salad of braised fennel with thyme, feta, and grilled chorizo

> 10 oz small fennel bulbs > 3 pinches thyme flowers > 2 tablespoons olive oil > 16 slices chorizo > 3 tablespoons balsamic vinegar > 4–6 feta cheese > 1 handful arugula leaves > sea salt <

• Preheat the oven to 400°F. • Rinse and quarter the fennel bulbs, then arrange them in a gratin dish. • Sprinkle with thyme flowers, drizzle over

Hot tip

Baby fennel, eaten raw like a radish, with a sprinkle of salt and a little fresh butter, or dipped in fromage blanc seasoned with curry powder— a true delight!

1 tablespoon olive oil and season with salt. • Cover with aluminum foil and bake in the preheated oven for 30 minutes. • Meanwhile, dry-fry the chorizo in a pan until slightly crisp. • Remove the fennel from the oven and tip into a salad bowl. • Sprinkle with balsamic vinegar and top with the desired amount of feta cheese cut into cubes. • Add the chorizo slices, finishing off with the arugula. • Lastly, drizzle over the remaining tablespoon of olive oil.

+ The arugula adds a wonderful peppery flavor to this recipe. Serve the salad as an appetizer, or as a light supper dish.

Raw fennel and orange salad

> 2 fennel bulbs > 2 oranges > 2 parsley sprigs, plus extra for garnish > grain mustard > 1 tablespoon wholegrain mustard (moutarde à l'ancienne) > 1 tablespoon sherry vinegar > 3 tablespoons light vegetable oil > ½ cup pine nuts (or walnut kernels) > salt and freshly ground black pepper <

• Rinse the fennel bulbs and slice thinly. • Peel the oranges and free the segments from their pith and membranes, or cut the segments into small pieces. • Coarsely chop the parsley. • Prepare a vinaigrette by combining both mustards, the vinegar, and oil. • Season with salt and pepper. • Add the pine nuts or walnut kernels for crunch, and a few parsley sprigs for color.

+ A delicious sweet-savory salad with an added nutty crunch.

"Carpaccio" of marinated raw fennel

> 1 fennel bulb > 3 tablespoons olive oil > 4 tablespoons lemon juice > olives <

• Rinse and drain the fennel. • Cut into wafer-thin slices. • Arrange the fennel slices on a serving plate and drizzle with the olive oil and lemon juice. • Marinate for 1 hour. • Add the olives and serve.

+ A speedy recipe that goes really well with smoked salmon.

Quick fennel risotto

> 4 onions > 4 small fennel bulbs > 7 tablespoons olive oil > 1¼ cups risotto rice > 1 chicken bouillon cube, dissolved in 3 cups boiling water > 4 tablespoons freshly grated Parmesan cheese <

• Peel the onions and slice into rounds. • Rinse the fennel bulbs and cut into small dice. • Cook the onions in 3 tablespoons olive oil until soft, then add the fennel and rice. • When the rice grains turn pearly white, add the chicken bouillon all at once, cover, and cook over a low heat, stirring occasionally, until the liquid is entirely absorbed. • Just before serving, stir in the remaining olive oil and add the grated Parmesan cheese.

+ With a real risotto, you need to add the hot bouillon gradually, and stir constantly. This simplified version gives a similar result for a lot less effort.

Like garlic and onions, the leek is a bulb plant; however, it differs from its cousins in having a reduced bulb and an elongated, white shaft that the botanists are constantly improving. Leeks are often referred to as "poor man's asparagus," yet they have their own nobility, offering a wide range of delicate flavors: from the mild sweetness of the white to the gutsier flavors of the green, the leek continues to exert its charm.

Leeks, a user's guide

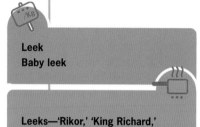

Leek
Baby leek

Leeks—'Rikor,' 'King Richard,' 'Laura': Production of these is spread out from September to April, depending on the maturing time of the different varieties. Only those varieties harvested in the depths of winter command outrageously high prices, but their taste has nothing to do with it: it's simply that, when the ground is frozen, the leeks can't be pulled and become scarcer!

Baby leeks: Like all mini vegetables, these are very mild, and all parts are edible.

> **Choosing for quality**
Choose leeks with very fresh, crisp leaf ends and very moist, flexible rootlets.
Ideal size: The younger and smaller, the better.
Bad sign: Dried out leaves and roots? Change your supplier!

> **Storage**
It's best to store leeks green leaves, roots and all, and prepare them only at the last minute. They keep relatively well for up to one week in a cool place (a window sill or the corner of a balcony suits them very well, as frost doesn't harm them).

> **Preparation**
Washing This is a crucial, delicate stage requiring technique and thoroughness, since nothing is more unpleasant than crunching on residual sand. First, cut off as much of the green part as you don't want, then cut off the roots and hold the leek with its bulb pointing upward from this point on. Now remove the outside leaf envelope, which can be a bit tough, and, using a sharp knife, split the whole leek from the center of the white up to the end of the green leaves, but not quite through. Finally, wash thoroughly under running water, fanning each leaf section out to loosen any earth or grit.

Calendar

Energy
25 kcal per 100 g

Nutritional advantages
The green of the leek is rich in vitamin C and pro-vitamin A (carotene), while the white is a treasure trove of vitamins B and PP. Leeks are high in fiber and have a diuretic effect. They are reputed to be excellent for clearing up singers' and speakers' voice problems.

Leeks are always eaten cooked, either as an onion substitute to flavor a dish, or as a garnish in their own right. They are also used to advantage in a number of soups, broths, stew, and mixed-vegetable stir-fries.

Leeks, simplicity itself

Leeks vinaigrette

> 2 leeks > classic vinaigrette dressing (*see recipe p. 145*) > sea salt <

• Wash the leeks thoroughly. • Boil them in salted water, then drain. • Dress with a really mustardy vinaigrette.

✚ The leeks may also be boiled in a bouillon to add flavor. Remove them from the pan as soon as they're tender and drain them well before dressing. You could garnish the leeks vinaigrette with a chopped shallot and a finely grated hard-cooked egg.

Braised leek chunks

> 8 leeks, white part only > 1½ tablespoons butter > balsamic vinegar > walnut (or hazelnut or sesame) oil > salt <

• Wash the leeks thoroughly, discarding the green part • Cut the leeks on the slant into 3-inch chunks. • Heat the butter in a skillet and add the leeks. • Moisten with about ¾ cup water, season with salt and simmer, covered, for 40 minutes, until all the liquid has been absorbed. • Prepare a vinaigrette dressing with the balsamic vinegar and the oil of your choice as an accompaniment.

 Serve as a vegetable side dish with the vinaigrette dressing on the side, with broiled meat, for example.

Leeks with saffron

> 16 small leeks > 3 oz butter > ⅔ cup white wine > 1 pinch saffron threads

• Preheat the oven to 300°F. • Wash leeks carefully and arrange them on the base of a gratin dish. • Melt the butter in a small pan and add the white wine and saffron threads. • Pour this mixture over the leeks, then cover them with aluminum foil and bake in the preheated oven for 40 minutes.

✚ The simple, homely leek paired with sophisticated saffron—a bold and delightful partnership that you and your family are just bound to love!

Leek and potato soup

> 2 leeks > 4 potatoes > 1 oz butter > salt and freshly ground black pepper <

• Wash the leeks thoroughly and cut them into thick slices. • Peel the potatoes and shred on the coarse side of a grater. • Sweat the vegetables in butter in a large stewpot or flameproof casserole dish. • Moisten with 6 cups water or chicken bouillon made with a cube, season with salt and pepper and simmer for 45 minutes (or for 15 minutes in a pressure cooker).

✚ For a sure hit with the kids, replace the potatoes with two handfuls of alphabet pasta. Try this also as a vichyssoise, simply cooking only the white part of the leeks in milk rather than water, then blending in an electric blender until smooth and serving chilled, sprinked with a few finely chopped chives.

Hot tip

On the day following a holiday, after a bowl of broth made from leeks—I'm ready to face the fray again!

"Melted" leeks with crème fraîche

> 4 leeks > 1½ tablespoons butter > 2 tablespoons crème fraîche or thick yogurt > salt and freshly ground black pepper <

• Trim the leeks, carefully wash and cut them into thin slices. • Heat the butter in a pan and gently simmer the leeks, covered, for 40 minutes (moisten with a little water if the leeks show sign of sticking). • Season with salt and pepper and then stir in the crème fraîche.

✚ Serve as a tasty accompaniment to meat or fish dishes.

Pasta with leeks and gorgonzola cheese

> 4 leeks > 1½ tablespoons butter > 2 tablespoons crème fraîche or thick yogurt > 1¼ cups crumbled gorgonzola cheese > 14 oz pasta > salt and freshly ground black pepper <

• Make "melted" leeks as in the previous recipe. • Add the gorgonzola cheese and mix thoroughly so that the sauce is properly bound together before it is tossed with the pasta. • Cook the pasta in plenty of boiling salted water until just tender, drain, and add to the leek sauce.

✚ Serve with an arugula salad dressed with balsamic vinegar and olive oil.

Leek and smoked haddock quiche

> 10 oz leeks > 5 oz smoked haddock > 1 oz butter > 3 eggs > 3 tablespoons crème fraîche or thick yogurt > ¾ cup milk > pepper (or chili powder) > 1 batch plain pastry (*see recipe p. 146*) <

• Preheat the oven to 350°F. • Carefully wash the leeks and cut them into thick slices. • Cut the haddock into cubes. • Microwave the leek and haddock in the butter for 7 minutes. • In a large bowl, beat the eggs with the crème fraîche, milk, and pepper or chili powder (check before you add any salt as the smoked haddock is probably already salty enough). • Roll out and line a quiche pan with the pastry, spread the leeks and haddock over the base, and pour in the egg mixture. • Bake in the preheated oven for about 35 minutes.

✚ You can serve this quiche hot or just warmed with a green salad.

Stir-fried chicken and leeks

> 3 boneless chicken breasts > 3 tablespoons soy sauce > 3 tablespoons dry white wine > 2 teaspoons sugar > 2 tablespoons lemon juice > 1 pinch grated ginger > 4 leeks > 2 tablespoons olive oil <

• Cut the chicken into strips and place on a deep plate. • Sprinkle over the soy sauce, white wine, sugar, lemon juice, and ginger. • Stir well and leave to marinate in the refrigerator for at least an hour. • Remove and discard the green parts of the leeks, then wash the white parts thoroughly and cut on the slant into chunks. • Heat the olive oil in a wok or large skillet and stir-fry the leeks in their marinade over a high heat for 10 minutes.

✚ Alternatively, you could thread the chicken pieces onto skewers and barbecue them. In this case, cut the chicken pieces a bit bigger, and marinate them for a little longer.

Long the sole province of Chinese cuisine, beansprouts were confined to spring rolls and other Far Eastern dishes. The shoots are sprouted from a close relative of our haricot bean—the mung bean—which has been cultivated in India, China and Japan since the dawn of time—for 13,000 years, no less. A cross between a green vegetable and a pulse, their high protein and vitamin levels are unequalled among vegetables.

Beansprouts,
a user's guide

There is just one variety, sprouted from mung beans

Mung-bean sprouts: Found on the fresh-produce shelves, in small containers or bagged in the chill-cabinet, to be eaten raw or cooked.

> **Choosing for quality**
Choose very white, firm sprouts with a tightly closed seedhead, as these are signs of quality and crunchiness.
Ideal size: None.
Bad sign: If the seedheads are turning brown, walk on by.

> **Storage**
Keep beansprouts in a cool place for no more than a few days—otherwise they lose their crunchiness.

> **Preparation**
Washing Give the sprouts a quick dip in cold water, then drain thoroughly before using them.

Calendar

Energy
13 kcal per 100 g

Nutritional advantages
Beansprouts are exceptionally rich in protein and B vitamins.

Mung beans are soaked in pure water and kept in a dark, damp environment; in a few days, they grow crunchy little shoots. The starch from these beans is made into the famous Chinese vermicelli, or bean-thread noodles. Beansprouts are available year round, but it's in the fall and winter that our bodies derive the greatest benefit from them.

Beansprouts, simplicity itself

Chicken and beansprout salad

> 10 oz beansprouts > 2 boneless chicken breasts > 1 onion > 1 tablespoon soy sauce > 2 tablespoons olive oil > 1 tablespoon sesame oil <

• Rinse the beansprouts under cold water, drain well and place in a salad bowl. • Cut the chicken breasts into pieces and lightly fry in oil, or (if you are watching the calories) poach in a little chicken bouillon. • Peel the onion and slice into rounds. • Add the chicken and onion to the beansprouts. • In a bowl, whisk together the soy sauce and both the oils. • Pour this dressing over the salad and toss well.

✛ Serve, if if you prefer, sprinkled with a tablespoon of sesame seeds, dry-fried in a pan to bring out their flavor.

Beef and beansprout stir-fry

> 1 lb beansprouts > 1¼ lb broiling steak (sirloin, fillet, tenderloin, etc.) > 1 garlic clove > 1 shallot > 1 small piece fresh ginger > ½ bunch chives > oil for stir-frying > 2 tablespoons soy sauce <

• Rinse the beansprouts under cold water and drain. • Thinly cut the beef into strips (or have your butcher do this for you). • Chop the garlic clove and shallot, peel and grate the ginger, and finely chop the chives.• Heat a little oil in a wok. Sear the meat with the chopped garlic, remove from the wok with a slotted spoon and set aside to keep warm, but not hot or it will overcook. • Stir-fry the ginger, shallot, and chives in the meat juices until softened. • Tip in the beansprouts and cook until the water clinging to them has evaporated, then add the soy sauce. Return the meat to the wok and combine.

✛ You can bring the wok straight to the table to serve. This is a complete and balanced meal in itself.

Stir-fried chicken with beansprouts, mushrooms, bell pepper, and onion

> 1 lb beansprouts > oil for stir-frying > 1¼ lb boneless chicken (or turkey) breast > 1 garlic clove > 1 onion > 1 small piece fresh ginger > 4 large cultivated mushrooms > ½ green bell pepper > 2 tablespoons soy sauce <

• Rinse the beansprouts under cold water and drain. • Thinly slice the chicken (or turkey) breast into strips. • Chop the garlic and finely slice the onion. • Peel and grate the ginger. • Wipe and slice the mushrooms and rinse and slice the green pepper. • Heat some oil in a wok. Sear the meat with the chopped garlic, then set aside. • Stir-fry the onion, ginger, mushrooms, and bell pepper in the meat juices until softened. • Tip in the beansprouts and cook until the water clinging to them has evaporated, then add the soy sauce. • Mix well to combine.

✛ You can substitute carrots for the mushrooms in this recipe.

Shrimp and beansprout salad

> 1 lb beansprouts > 16 large cooked shrimp, > ¼ cucumber > 1 carrot > 1 tablespoon soy sauce > 1 tablespoon balsamic vinegar > 1 teaspoon mustard > 3 tablespoons olive oil <

• Rinse the beansprouts under cold water, then drain and transfer to a large bowl. • Peel the shrimp, discard the heads, and add the shrimp to the beansprouts. • Thinly slice the cucumber;

Hot tip

Fresh, raw beansprouts, mixed into a vegetable stir-fry, add extra crunch.

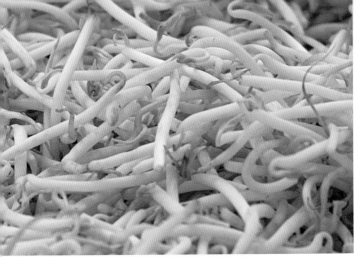

cut the carrot into matchstick-sized pieces and add both to the salad. • In a bowl, whisk together the soy sauce, balsamic vinegar, mustard, and olive oil; pour this dressing over the salad and toss well.

✛ Serve sprinkled with finely chopped chives, or scallions sliced as thinly as possible.

Red mullet, beansprout, and sun-dried tomato salad

> 1 lb beansprouts > 4 sun-dried tomatoes > 1 tablespoon soy sauce > 1 tablespoon balsamic vinegar > 5 tablespoons olive oil > 8 red mullet fillets (have your fishman do the filleting) <

• Rinse the beansprouts under cold water; drain them well and place in a salad bowl. • Cut the sun-dried tomatoes into small dice and add to the salad bowl. • In a bowl, whisk together the soy sauce, balsamic vinegar and 3 tablespoons of the olive oil. • Pour the dressing over the beansprouts and toss well. • Pan-fry the fish fillets in the remaining olive oil. • Arrange over the salad and serve.

✛ Serve as an appetizer or main course, depending on your appetite (and the size of the fish fillets).

Crab, carrot, and beansprout omelet

> 5 oz beansprouts > 1 carrot > 1 shallot > olive oil for cooking > 5 oz canned crabmeat, flaked > 6 eggs > milk > salt and freshly ground black pepper <

• Rinse the beansprouts under cold water and drain well. • Peel and grate the carrot. • Finely slice the shallot and sauté in hot olive oil in a skillet until golden. • Tip the beansprouts and grated carrot into the pan and stir-fry for 5 minutes; add the drained, flaked

crabmeat. • Beat the eggs with a fork in a large bowl and add the milk (quantity as required). • Season with salt and pepper. • Tip the contents of the skillet into the bowl and stir together. • Heat another tablespoon of olive oil in the pan, pour in the egg mixture and make an omelet, cooking until the egg has set but not gone dry.

✛ East and West meet in this recipe to produce a beautiful and delicious dish.

Duck breasts with beansprouts

> 2 duck breasts > five-spice powder > 14 oz beansprouts > 2 tablespoons shoyu (Japanese soy sauce) > salt <

• Preheat the oven to 425°F. • Sprinkle the skin of the duck breasts with a little five-spice powder and salt. • Arrange the duck breasts in an ovenproof dish, skin side up, and cook in the preheated oven (or on the barbecue) for 10 minutes. • Rinse the beansprouts, then blanch for 1 minute in boiling salted water. • Thoroughly drain and place on a serving dish and season with the shoyu. • Carve the duck breasts in thin slices and arrange on the bed of beansprouts before serving.

✛ Five-spice powder is a mixture of star anise, cinnamon, fennel, cloves, and Szechuan pepper. Japanese soy sauce is more aromatic than the Chinese variety, but either version can be used in this recipe.

winter

VEGETABLES

Regarded as a vegetable in some parts of the world and a fruit in others, the avocado has a fleshy, melting texture and a nutty flavor that places it midway between "sweet" and "savory." Once the sacred fruit and a symbol of life for the Aztecs and Mayas of South America, the avocado was introduced into Europe by the Spanish in the 17th century. However, it is only in the last 20 years that it has become widely available and now forms the basis of a number of savory dishes and desserts.

Avocados,
a user's guide

Haas avocado
Fuerte avocado
Ettinger avocado

Haas avocado: Has a thick, pebbly, purplish brown skin and the tastiest flesh.

Fuerte and Ettinger avocados: Have a smoother, medium green skin. They are also smoother in the mouth, with a milder flavor than Haas.

> **Choosing for quality**

Avocados are at their tastiest just before they are fully ripe. Test for ripeness by lightly pressing the fruit stalk—if the flesh yields to gentle pressure, the fruit is fully ripe. Always choose avocados with a firm fruit stalk and leave them to ripen for a few days at a temperature of 53–59°F. You can speed up the process by wrapping them in newspaper.

Ideal size: None.

Bad signs: If avocados are soft, it means they have been roughly handled, which is disastrous. If there is a dark mark around the fruit stalk, the avocado is overripe. Bruises and dark, sunken spots on the skin are also a bad sign.

> **Storage**

Unripe avocados keep for up to 5 days at room temperature, and 2–3 days in the vegetable compartment of the refrigerator.

> **Preparation**

To prevent the flesh discoloring add lemon juice and, strange as it may seem, leave the pit in the fruit or the avocado mixture until ready to serve.

Calendar

Energy
220 kcal per 100g
(the flesh is rich in lipids—22%)

Nutritional advantages
Large quantities of potassium and magnesium (good for the nervous system), vitamin C (prevents stress and fatigue) and vitamin A.

Avocados are usually sold ten days after being picked—this makes sure that the fruit is slightly underripe when purchased and finishes ripening in the home. Avocados are always eaten raw and go well with tomatoes, limes, lemons, fresh cilantro, pimentos, grapefruit and all kinds of seafood. If you are watching your weight, there's no need to add oil—lemon juice and a little salt and pepper work just as well.

Avocados, simplicity itself

Avocados with lemon juice and crab pieces

> 5 oz crab pieces > 4 tablespoons lemon juice > 4 avocados > mayonnaise (optional) > tomato ketchup (optional) > Tabasco (optional) > cognac (optional) > salt and freshly ground black pepper <

• Mix the crab pieces, lemon juice together in a bowl and season with salt and pepper. • Halve the avocados and fill each half with the crab mixture. • For gourmets only: add fresh mayonnaise or 'cocktail' sauce (mayonnaise plus 2 tablespoons tomato ketchup, a few drops of Tabasco and 1 teaspoon cognac).

+ Halve the avocados at the last minute to prevent the flesh discolouring. Fresh shrimp can be used instead of crab pieces.

Chilled avocado soup with cilantro and lime

> 2 avocados > 10 fresh cilantro leaves > grated rind and juice of $\frac{1}{2}$ lime > 1 chicken bouillon cube, dissolved in 2 cups cold water > $\frac{2}{3}$ cup light cream > Tabasco > salt and freshly ground black pepper <

• Peel the avocados and, using an electric blender, purée the flesh with 8 of the cilantro leaves. • Pour the mixture into a serving bowl. • Add the lime juice, chicken bouillon, light cream, and a few drops of Tabasco, to taste. • Mix well and season to taste. • Shred the remaining cilantro leaves and use to garnish the soup, together with the grated lime zest. • Serve well chilled.

+ Add a few steamed Dublin Bay prawns and you have a dish fit for a king.

Avocado sorbet and smoked salmon

> 2 ripe avocados > juice of 2 limes > $\frac{3}{4}$ cup white wine > $1\frac{1}{4}$ cups water > $2\frac{1}{2}$ tablespoons sugar > slices of smoked salmon, to serve <

• Peel the avocados and purée the flesh in an electric blender. • Pour the mixture into a large mixing bowl. • Stir in the lime juice, white wine, measured water, and sugar, and mix well. • Churn in an ice-cream maker or place in a suitable container in the freezer and freeze, breaking up the ice crystals with a fork every 15 minutes. • The finished sorbet should have smooth, creamy texture.

+ Serve the sorbet with slices of smoked salmon.

Guacamole

> 4 salad onions or scallions > 2 tomatoes > 4 cilantro sprigs > 1 small chile > 2 avocados > juice of 1 lemon > walnut bread, to serve <

• Thinly slice the onions; rinse and dice the tomatoes. • Shred the cilantro sprigs and cut the chile into fine strips. • Peel the avocados and mash the flesh with a fork in a bowl. • Add the lemon juice, sliced onions, diced tomatoes, shredded cilantro, and strips of chile. • Mix thoroughly.

+ Serve on toasted walnut bread—it makes a delicious change from corn chips.

Hot tip

Haas, with its nutty flavor, is by far the best variety.

-20 Avocado salad with romaine lettuce and broiled bacon

> 2 avocados > 2 romaine lettuce hearts > vinaigrette (*see recipe p. 145*) > strong mustard > 8 slices smoked bacon, thinly sliced > 4 tablespoons pine nuts <

• Peel the avocados and cut into eight. • Rinse and quarter the lettuce hearts. • Prepare a vinaigrette adding strong mustard. • Brown the bacon slices under the broiler. • Lightly toast the pine nuts in a dry pan. • Mix the ingredients carefully in a salad bowl, taking care not to crush the avocado pieces.

+ Walnuts can be used instead of pine nuts. The nuts complement the nutty flavor of the avocados.

Chilled avocado soup with salad onions and spinach shoots

> 2 avocados > 4 salad onions with stems, chopped > 1 lb young spinach, chopped > 1 chicken bouillon cube, dissolved in 2 cups cold water > 1 tablespoon Worcesteshire sauce > grapefruit, to garnish (optional) <

• Peel the avocados and, using an electric blender, purée the flesh with the onions, onion stems, and spinach. • Add the chicken bouillon and Worcestershire sauce. • Mix well. • Serve chilled.

+ You can garnish the soup with a slice of peeled grapefruit.

Today, there are a dozen or so edible varieties of cabbage, divided into three main categories. The first—the headed or ball-headed cabbage—includes the smooth, green summer and winter cabbages, the crinkly, dark green Savoy, the white Dutch cabbage, red cabbage, and Brussels sprouts. The second category includes the conical and non-heading cabbages (e.g. the Chinese and "tenderheart" cabbages), while the third comprises cabbages whose flowers (florets) are eaten rather than the leaves—cauliflower, broccoli, and Romanseco (a type of broccoli).

Cabbages, a user's guide

Smooth, green cabbage (round-headed cabbage); **Crinkly, green cabbage; Crinkly, dark green cabbage (Savoy); White or Dutch cabbage; Red cabbage; Chinese cabbage; Brussels sprouts; Cauliflower; Romanesco; Broccoli**

Smooth, green cabbage: Used for stuffed cabbage leaves; in stews and farmhouse soups. It can also be eaten raw, when young, with vinaigrette.

Crinkly, green cabbage: Has tender, white inner leaves in a compact head.

Crinkly, dark green cabbage (Savoy): Midway between the smooth, green cabbage and the crinkly green cabbage, it reduces by half in cooking.

White cabbage: Used for making sauerkraut and coleslaw.

Red cabbage: An almost purple, headed cabbage eaten raw or cooked, in a salad or as an accompaniment. It can also be pickled in vinegar.

Chinese cabbage: Eaten raw or cooked, simply tossed in butter.

Brussels sprouts: Have a tendency to break down during cooking.

Cauliflower: Available from June–December.

Romanesco: Milder and sweeter than cauliflower, popular with children.

Broccoli: The florets cook very quickly but the stems (which should be peeled if thick) take a little longer.

> **Choosing for quality**
Choose heavy, compact cabbages, with crisp, bright green leaves and tightly packed hearts.
Ideal size: None.
Bad signs: Yellowing leaves edged with brown mean the cabbage is far from fresh. In the case of broccoli, open florets are a sign that it is well past its best.

> **Storage**
Cabbages store well—from a few days in the vegetable compartment of the refrigerator for smaller ones, up to a month for larger cabbages.

> **Preparation**

Green, white, red and Chinese cabbages, and Brussels sprouts
Before you start Discard the tough, and sometimes dirty, outer leaves and stalk.
Washing Cut out the large veins and wash the remaining leaves.
Blanching green cabbages If you are going to eat cooked green cabbage, blanching in boiling salted water for 5 minutes eliminates some of the volatile sulfur compounds that have an adverse effect on some people. Adding a chunk or crust of bread to the water at the same time as the cabbage is a very effective way of preventing the cooking odor from permeating the house. The bread also gives the cabbage a more subtle flavor.

Cauliflower, Romanesco and broccoli
Before you start Discard the outer leaves, stalk and any tough stems.
Washing Remove and wash the florets. Peel broccoli stalks, if necessary, like carrots and cook for one-third longer than the florets. Cut through the stalks if thick, this speeds up cooking.

Calendar

Energy
Per 100 g: 24 kcal for green cabbage; 10 kcal for cauliflower; 20 kcal for broccoli.

Nutritional advantages
Green cabbage is particularly rich in fiber, Provitamin A and Vitamins C, B9 (for red corpuscles) and E. It also contains sulfur and large quantities of calcium.

Like potatoes, cabbage goes well with everything. It can be served cooked and tender or raw and crunchy. It is a traditional accompaniment for pork and other roast meats but also goes well with fish.

Green, red, and white cabbage, simplicity itself

Red cabbage vinaigrette with apples and raisins

> ½ red cabbage > 2 tablespoons raisins > 2 apples > vinaigrette (*see recipe p. 145*) > olive oil > lemon juice <

• Discard the outer leaves and thick core of the cabbage, shred the remaining cabbage. • Soak the raisins in a little warm water. • Peel the apples and slice thinly. • Put the cabbage and apple into a salad bowl. • In another bowl, prepare a vinaigrette with the olive oil and lemon juice to taste. • Mix the vinaigrette into the cabbage and apple; drain the raisins well and add to the salad. • Toss the salad before serving.

✚ This recipe works just as well with a small white cabbage and a traditional vinaigrette made with plenty of mustard.

Buttery cooked green cabbage and potatoes

> 1 green cabbage > 4 large potatoes > a crust or chunk of bread (optional) > 4 oz butter > salt <

• Discard the outer leaves of the cabbage, cut out the large veins and wash the remaining leaves. Cut the heart into quarters. • Peel the potatoes. • Plunge the vegetables (and a chunk of bread if required) into a pan of boiling salted water. • Cook for 20 minutes and drain. • Return the cabbage and potatoes to the pan, add knobs of butter and mash with a fork over a low heat.

✚ Serve as an accompaniment for meats such as roast pork or veal.

Braised green cabbage with juniper, carrots, and diced bacon

> 1 green cabbage > a crust or chunk of bread (optional) > 1 carrot > 1 onion > 2 garlic cloves > 8 juniper berries > 2 cups diced bacon > 1 bouquet garni (parsley, thyme, bay) > 2 cups water > salt and freshly ground black pepper <

• Discard the outer leaves of the cabbage, cut out the large veins and wash the remaining leaves. Cut the heart into quarters. • Plunge the cabbage (and a chunk of bread if required) into a pan of boiling salted water and cook for 5 minutes. • Drain and then plunge the cabbage into iced water to fix its green color. Drain once more. • Peel the carrot and cut into rounds, peel and slice the onion, peel and crush the garlic, lightly crush the juniper berries. • Brown the diced bacon in a Dutch oven and add the cabbage, carrot, onion, garlic, juniper berries, and bouquet garni. • Season lightly and add the measured water. • Cover and cook for 1 hour over a low heat.

✚ Serve as an accompaniment for roast poultry. This recipe works just as well with Brussels sprouts, but remember to halve the cooking time.

-20 Microwaved cabbage leaves with butter and breadcrumbs

> 4 good cabbage leaves > a knob of butter > 1 tablespoon breadcrumbs <

• Wash and shred the cabbage leaves. • Arrange on a microwave-proof plate, add the knob of butter and sprinkle with the breadcrumbs. • Cover and microwave according to maker's instructions for 5 minutes.

Cabbage soup

> ½ green cabbage > 2 tablespoons goose fat, or butter > 2 garlic cloves > 2 turnips > 2 carrots > 4 potatoes > 2 thick slices bacon, cut into pieces > 1 bouquet garni > 8 cups cold water > salt and freshly ground black pepper > Roquefort cheese (optional), to garnish <

• Discard the outer leaves of the cabbage, cut out the large veins and wash the remaining leaves. Cut the heart into quarters and shred the heart and leaves. • Brown the shredded cabbage in the goose fat, or butter in a Dutch oven. • Peel and crush the garlic and add to the pan. • Peel the turnips, carrots, and potatoes, cut into pieces and add to the cabbage, along with the bacon pieces. • Add the measured water and bouquet garni. • Season to taste and leave to simmer gently or 1 hour.

✚ Serve in a soup tureen with slices of baguette or crusty bread and perhaps topped with a sprinkling of crumbled Roquefort cheese.

Coleslaw

> ¼ white cabbage > 2 carrots > mayonnaise (see recipe p. 147) > 1 tablespoon light cream > 1 tablespoon cider vinegar > 2 tablespoons lemon juice <

• Thinly slice the white cabbage, rinse and drain well. • Peel and grate the carrots. • Place the vegetables in a salad bowl. • Use another bowl to prepare the mayonnaise, using plenty of mustard. • Add the single cream, cider vinegar and lemon juice. • Mix well and add to the vegetables in the salad bowl.

✚ Served with hamburgers, this "almost" makes a balanced meal, provided you don't overdo the mayonnaise.

Chinese cabbage and mushrooms à la japonaise

> 8 oz packet Japanese egg noodles > 14 oz Chinese cabbage > 14 oz cultivated mushrooms > 1 red onion > 1 garlic clove > oil for cooking > 4 tablespoons soy sauce > sesame seeds, chives or scallions, to garnish <

• Cook the noodles as directed on the packet. • Thinly shred the cabbage and cut the mushrooms into thin slices, rinse and drain. • Peel and chop the onion and garlic, and then sautée with the vegetables in an oiled skillet or wok. • Add the drained noodles and the soy sauce.

✚ Serve sprinkled with sesame seeds and chopped chives or scallions.

Stir-fried green cabbage, leek, and fillet of duck à l'orange

> ½ green cabbage > 2 leeks, white part only > 2 duck breasts > grated rind of 1 orange > salt and freshly ground black pepper <

• Discard the outer leaves of the cabbage, cut out the large veins and wash the remaining cabbage. Cut the heart into quarters and shred the heart and leaves. • Rinse and shred the leeks. • Cut the duck breasts into slices about ¼ inch thick and brown in a wok without oil. • Remove from the wok and keep warm. • Discard half the meat juices and brown all the vegetables in the remaining juices. • Season to taste with salt and pepper and then stir in the duck slices and grated orange rind.

✚ A wok enables you to cook the sliced duck breasts quickly and prevents them drying out too much in the center. If you use a pan, you may have to cook them in several batches.

Cauliflower and Romanesco are prepared in much the same way and can be eaten raw or cooked rapidly. Broccoli shouldn't be cooked for too long (no more than 8 minutes), to make the most of its crunchy texture. There are two types of broccoli—the compact "heading (or cauliflower) broccoli" and the more branching "sprouting broccoli"—see "Did you know?" below.

Cauliflower, Romanesco, and broccoli, simplicity itself

Cauliflower and potatoes au gratin

> 1 cauliflower > a crust or chunk of bread (optional) > 4 potatoes > 2 eggs > ²⁄₃ cup light cream > pinch of grated nutmeg > 1 cup grated Gruyère cheese > salt and freshly ground black pepper > turmeric (optional) <

• Preheat the oven to 375°F. • Discard the leaves and stalk of the cauliflower and separate the florets. • Rinse the florets, then plunge into boiling salted water and cook for 15 minutes with a chunk of bread, if using. • Peel the potatoes and cook in a second pan of boiling salted water. • Drain the cauliflower and potatoes, and mash the potatoes with a fork or potato masher. Add the cauliflower to the mashed potatoes. • Beat the eggs, cream, and nutmeg together. • Season to taste and add to the vegetables. • Place in a gratin dish. • Sprinkle with the Gruyère cheese and bake in the preheated oven for 20 minutes, or until the topping is crisp and golden.

✚ Add a teaspoon of turmeric for a little touch of sunshine.

Puréed broccoli

> 1 broccoli head > ¹⁄₂ cup olive oil > 3¹⁄₂ tablespoons walnut, hazelnut or sesame oil > salt <

• Discard the broccoli leaves. Separate the florets, peel and cut the stalk if necessary and rinse well. • Plunge the stalk into boiling salted water and cook for 5 minutes, then add the florets and cook until tender. • Drain and purée in an electric blender and add both types of oil. • Adjust seasoning to taste.

✚ This dish makes an ideal accompaniment for fish or broiled meat.

Pasta with broccoli, pecorino, and goat's cheese

> 1 broccoli head > 14 oz pasta > 1 cup crumbled goat's cheese > ¹⁄₂ cup grated pecorino cheese (or Parmesan, if preferred) > 2 tablespoons olive oil > 1 handful pine nuts, lightly toasted (optional) > salt and freshly ground black pepper <

• Discard the leaves and stalk of the broccoli, separate the florets and rinse well. • Cook the pasta in a large pan of boiling salted water and, 8 minutes before the end of the cooking time, add the broccoli florets. • Drain the pasta and broccoli well and turn into a serving dish. • Add the two cheeses, drizzle with the olive oil, season to taste and sprinkle with the toasted pine nuts, if desired.

✚ Cooking the pasta and broccoli together saves time.

Cauliflower "couscous"

> 1 cauliflower > butter for cooking > 1 tablespoon *ras-al-hanout* (a Moroccan mix of ground spices: cloves, cinnamon, black pepper) > salt <

• Discard the leaves and stalk of the cauliflower and separate into florets. • Break down the florets in an electric blender to obtain a fine couscous-like grain. • Plunge the cauliflower 'couscous' into boiling salted water for 30 seconds and then drain well. • Brown in a greased skillet with the *ras-al-hanout* spice mixture.

✚ Serve the "couscous" with broiled merguez, or other spicy sausages, and a few steamed carrots and zucchini.

Romanesco with lemon juice and tarragon

> 2 Romanesco heads > a crust or chunk of bread (optional) > $\frac{1}{4}$ chicken bouillon cube, dissolved in $\frac{1}{2}$ cup warm water > grated rind and juice of 2 lemons > 3 oz butter > 1 tablespoon chopped tarragon leaves > $\frac{1}{2}$ cup grated Comté or Gruyère cheese > salt and freshly ground black pepper <

• Discard the Romanesco leaves, separate the florets and rinse well. • Plunge into boiling salted water and cook for 3 minutes with a crust or chunk of bread, if using. • Drain and plunge into iced water to fix the green color. • Pour the bouillon, grated rind, and lemon juice into a pan. • Bring to a boil, beat in the butter, and add the shredded tarragon, salt, and pepper. • Arrange the Romanesco in a gratin dish, cover with the sauce and sprinkle with the grated cheese. • Place under a medium broiler for 15 minutes until the top is crisp and golden and the center is heated through.

+ Serve with roast chicken delicately flavored with sprigs of fresh tarragon. A guaranteed success!

Cream of cauliflower soup

> 1 cauliflower > a crust or chunk of bread (optional) > $\frac{3}{4}$ cup light cream > $\frac{1}{2}$ cup milk > $\frac{1}{2}$ cup water > chicken bouillon cube > salt > ground ginger and chervil, to garnish <

• Discard the leaves and stalk of the cauliflower, separate into florets and rinse well. • Plunge into boiling salted water and cook for 5 minutes, with a crust or chunk of bread, if using. • Pour the light cream, milk, measured water, and bouillon cube into a high-sided skillet. • Drain the cauliflower and add to the skillet and cook gently for 15 minutes. • Blend the soup in an electric blender, adding more milk if necessary.

+ Flavor the soup with 1 tablespoon of freshly ground ginger and garnish with a few fresh chervil leaves, which have been shredded with scissors and added at the last minute.

WINTER VEGETABLES > cauliflower, Romanesco and broccoli

Carrots are available all year round, but their fine texture is at its best in winter. They can be eaten raw, cooked, with a main dish, an accompaniment, and even a dessert. There are a number of different summer and winter varieties, but consumers tend to divide them into two main categories—field-grown carrots that store well and the more delicate, slender carrots sold in bunches with their leaves. The latter are early varieties, cultivated under cover, available in May and September.

Carrots,
a user's guide

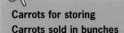

Carrots for storing
Carrots sold in bunches

Carrots for storing: Sold loose or packaged, these are a must in any vegetable rack throughout the entire year.

Carrots sold in bunches: Younger and sweeter, these are delicious raw and can be used in juice, grated, cut into sticks and served as an appetizer with a cream-cheese dip, or even in a dessert.

> **Choosing for quality**
Choose carrots with a good orange color and a smooth, unblemished skin with no cracks or bruises.
Ideal size: Carrots which are all the same size will benefit from having the same cooking time.
Bad signs: Withered skin is a sign of aging.

> **Storage**
Carrots will keep for at least a week in the vegetable compartment of the refrigerator, provided they are not stored in a plastic bag. Alternatively, store in a cool, well-ventilated place.

> **Preparation**
Peeling Peel all carrots apart from the carrots sold in bunches, which can be scrubbed like new potatoes. The latter will look more attractive if you leave on about 1 inch or so of the leaf stems.

Calendar

Energy
40 kcal per 100 g

Nutritional advantages
Carrots are rich in fiber. The carotene that gives them their color is transformed into Vitamin A. They also contain Vitamins B1, B2, and C, as well as potassium, calcium, magnesium, and iron. Carrots help reduce cholesterol and stimulate the immune system.

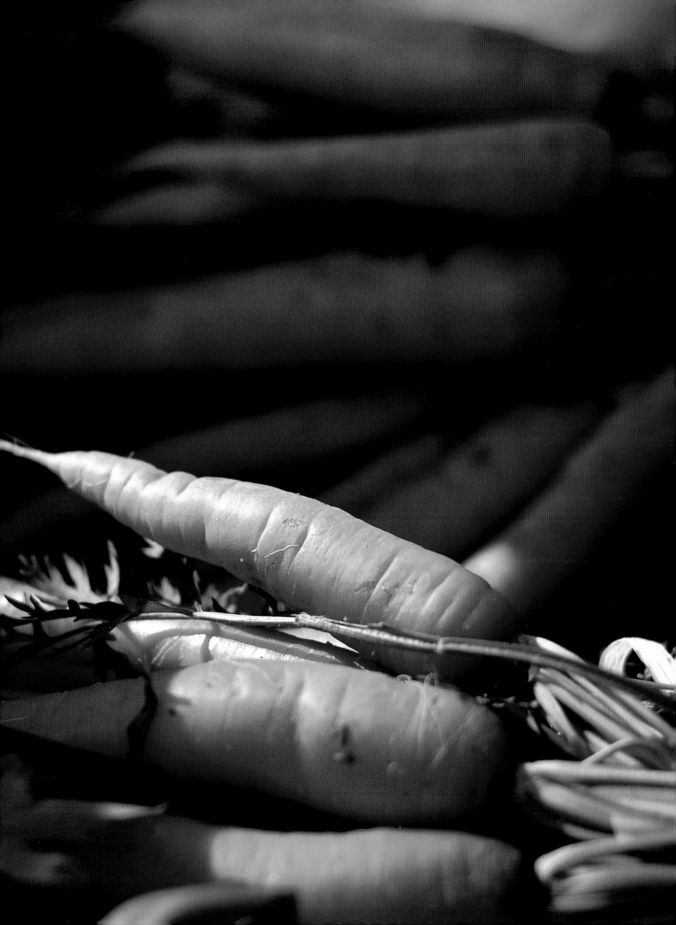

Carrots go with most ingredients—butter, crème fraîche or yogurt, olive oil, fish or meat—and all kinds of vegetables. Hot spices and the strong flavors of cumin or curry set them off to perfection, while green herbs complement their beautiful orange color.

Carrots, simplicity itself

Cream of grated carrot and zucchini

> 3 carrots > 1 zucchini > ¾ cup milk
> ½ vegetable bouillon cube <

• Peel and coarsely grate the carrots. • Grate the zucchini, using the same size grater. • Put the vegetables in a pan with the milk and ½ bouillon cube, and cook over a low heat for 10 minutes. • Serve warm.

+ A quick and easy—and extremely healthy —vegetable accompaniment.

Three Cs tagliatelle (carrots, curry and cilantro)

> 14 oz tagliatelle > 2 carrots > 1 oz butter
> 3 tablespoons light cream > 1 teaspoon curry powder > ½ bunch fresh cilantro, chopped > salt and freshly ground black pepper <

• Cook the pasta in a large pan of boiling salted water. • While it is cooking, peel the carrots and cut into thin strips with a paring knife or vegetable peeler. • Melt the butter in a high-sided skillet or wok and brown the carrot for 3–4 minutes. • Add the cream and curry powder and season to taste with salt and pepper. • When the pasta is ready, drain and add to the sauce, mixing well. • Add the chopped cilantro to the dish just before serving.

+ The attractive colors of this pasta dish also make it a feast for the eyes.

Carrot salad with sweet-and-sour sauce

> 4 carrots > 2 oz butter > 10 parsley sprigs, tied into a bunch with string > ½ cup sugar >
½ cup water > 2 tablespoons vinegar > salt and freshly ground black pepper > herbs, to garnish (optional) <

• Peel the carrots, cut into rounds and place in a pan. • Add the butter and parsley, and cover with cold water. • Season, bring to a boil and simmer over moderate heat for 5 minutes. • Drain the carrots but keep the cooking liquid. • Prepare a caramel with the sugar and measured water. • When it has a thick consistency, deglaze with the vinegar and add the cooking liquid from the carrots. • Leave to cool. • Season the carrots with the sweet-and-sour sauce and serve warm.

+ Sprinkle the salad with chopped parsley, cilantro or chives.

Cream of carrot soup with saffron

> 2 lb carrots > 1 potato > 1 oz butter >
2 chicken bouillon cubes, dissolved in 4 cups hot water > pinch of saffron threads > ⅔ cup light cream > salt and freshly ground black pepper > bacon and parings of orange rind, to garnish (optional) <

• Peel and thickly slice the carrots and potato. • Brown in the butter in a large pan. • Add the chicken bouillon and the saffron threads. • Season and simmer gently for 30 minutes. • Blend in an electric blender, add the cream and blend again until it is light and frothy.

+ Garnish the soup with dry-fried bacon bits and a sprinkle of orange rind to add a little zing.

Hot tip

To make carrot juice, put two large carrots in a juicer, measure the juice extracted and add another ⅓ orange juice, the grated rind of an orange and the juice of half a lemon. Served chilled, it's absolutely delicious!

Braised beef with carrots

> 2 lb braising beef > 2 lb carrots > 3 onions > butter
for cooking > ¾ cup white wine > ½ chicken bouillon
cube, dissolved in ¾ cup hot water > 1 bouquet garni
(parsley, thyme, bay) > salt and freshly ground black
pepper <

• Cut the beef into pieces, about 3 x 2 x ¾ inches in
size. • Peel and slice the carrots and onions. • Melt
some butter in a Dutch oven dish and cook the pieces
of beef and sliced onion for 5 minutes. • Add the white
wine and chicken bouillon. • Deglaze the cooking juices
with a wooden spatula, then add the sliced carrot and
bouquet garni. • Season and leave to cook on a low
heat for 1½ hours.

✚ This is a variation of the classic dish known as
boeuf à la mode.

Cooked carrot salad with cumin and fresh cilantro

> 4 carrots > ½ bunch fresh cilantro > 1 garlic
clove > 4 tablespoons olive oil > 1 teaspoon harissa
> ½ teaspoon ground cumin > salt <

• Peel the carrots and cut into thickish slices. • Chop
the cilantro and crush the garlic using a garlic crusher.
• Cook the sliced carrot in boiling salted water for
15 minutes—they should retain their crunchiness
(al dente). • Drain and turn into a salad bowl. • While
the carrots are cooking, prepare a dressing with the
olive oil, harissa, cumin, cilantro, and garlic. • Mix the
dressing with the carrots and marinate in the refrigerator
for 24 hours before serving, stirring occasionally.

✚ Harissa is a North African/Middle Eastern spicy
paste available in good supermarkets,
delicatessens, and speciality stores.

Tajine of carrots with chicken escalopes

> 6 carrots > 1 onion > ½ lemon > 2 tablespoons
capers > 5 fresh parsley sprigs, chopped > 4 chicken
escalopes > olive oil for cooking > freshly ground black
pepper <

• Preheat the oven to 350°F. • Peel and slice the
carrots and onion, and slice the lemon. • Mix the sliced
carrot, onion and lemon together in a bowl and add the
capers and parsley. • Sauté the chicken escalopes in
olive oil until both sides are golden brown. • Arrange
the escalopes in a tajine (a glazed earthenware dish
with a conical lid) or ovenproof dish, cover with the
vegetable mixture and season with pepper. • Cover
(with aluminum foil, if using a lidless ovenproof dish) and
cook in the preheated oven for 45 minutes.

✚ This Sicilian recipe is ideal for all seasons and
all occasions.

Glazed carrots with salad onions and chorizo

> 1 lb carrots > 1 bunch of salad onions, or scallions
> 4 garlic cloves > 1 oz butter > pinch of sugar
> ½ chorizo (a long, dry, spicy pork sausage) <

• Peel the carrots, onions, and garlic cloves, and slice
the carrots. • Melt the butter in a high-sided skillet and
brown the sliced carrots with the garlic cloves and
whole onions. • Add the sugar, cover and cook over
a low heat for 20 minutes. • While the carrots and
onions are cooking, peel the chorizo and cut into
rounds. • Add to the skillet and cook for a further
10 minutes.

✚ There's no need to season this dish, the chorizo
does it for you. Delicious with fillet of cod fried
in olive oil.

Cultivated Belgian endive, or witloof, was "invented" in 1850 when the head gardener at the Brussels Botanical Gardens had the idea of "earthing up" wild endive to keep it warm and protect it from the light. The new varieties that have appeared in recent years mean that endive is no longer always entirely white—it can also have red leaves. But whatever their color, these new varieties have lost much of their bitterness which is now concentrated in the conical base.

Belgian endive,
a user's guide

White-leaved endive
Red Verona endive
Red Treviso endive
Red Chiogga endive

White-leaved endive (e.g. Belgian endive): its white leaves are due to the practice of "earthing up" which means the endive grows in total darkness, although there are now non-forced varieties.

Red Verona endive; Red Treviso endive; Red Chiogga endive: these relatively mild, red-leaved Italian varieties are prepared in the same way as white-leaved endive.

> **Choosing for quality**
Choose heads that are firm and compact, (white, if the white-leaved variety) with tightly packed leaves.
Ideal size: None.
Bad signs: Bad signs: Endive that is withered, dull-looking, and soft is past its best. Leaves that have turned green in the light will have a more bitter taste.

> **Storage**
Endive is a fragile vegetable. Store in the vegetable compartment of the refrigerator, but don't keep for more that 4–5 days. Never expose endive to the light.

> **Preparation**
Washing Rinse the heads rapidly in cold water but don't leave to soak, as they will become bitter.
Peeling Simply remove the bitter conical base below the leaves—endive is really quick and easy to prepare.
Handy hint A squeeze of lemon juice ensures the endive stays white during cooking.

Calendar	Energy	Nutritional advantages
	15 kcal per 100 g (95% water).	Endive contains fiber, B vitamins, and mineral salts.

Chicory can be prepared in a number of different ways. Eaten raw in a salad, its bitter-sweet taste goes well with the strong flavour of Roquefort and other blue cheeses. When cooked, it is delicious sweetened with honey, but avoid boiling as you'll lose both the delicate flavour and the vitamins.

Chicory, simplicity itself

Quick braised chicory with bacon

> 60 g (2½ oz) bacon, diced > 1 kg (2 lb) chicory > 100 ml (3½ fl oz) white wine > 100 ml (3½ fl oz) water > 1 teaspoon cornflour, mixed to a paste with a little water > salt and freshly ground black pepper <

• Brown the diced bacon in a pressure cooker. This recipe can be made by the traditional method of cooking in a saucepan but the actual braising time will be 15 minutes. • Rinse the chicory and remove the bitter conical base. Cut into 2-cm (³⁄₄-inch) thick slices, add to the pressure cooker and leave to sweat. • Add the wine and measured water. Season to taste. • Close the pressure cooker and braise for 5 minutes at maker's recommended pressure. • Remove the lid and stir in the cornflour paste to thicken the liquid.

✚ As an alternative, replace the bacon with a fairly thick slice of uncooked, cured ham cut into diced pieces.

Chicory with orange and ginger

> 4 chicory heads > juice of 4 oranges > 2 tablespoons lemon juice > 1 teaspoon grated fresh ginger > 50 g (2oz) butter <

• Preheat the oven to 180°C (350°C), gas mark 4. • Rinse the chicory and remove the bitter conical base. Cut in half and arrange in a gratin dish. • Add the orange and lemon juice, and grated ginger. Dot with the butter. • Cover with baking foil and cook in the preheated oven for 45 minutes.

✚ Use a tablespoon of crushed coriander seeds as an alternative to the ginger. Serve as an accompaniment for meat or fish.

Chicory salad with apple, raisins, walnuts and blue cheese

> 2 tablespoons raisins > 4 chicory heads > 2 eating apples > 50–75 g (2–3 oz) walnuts > 75 g (3 oz) blue cheese > mustard > sherry vinegar > groundnut oil > walnut oil > salt and freshly ground black pepper <

• Soak the raisins in a little warm water. • Rinse the chicory and remove the bitter conical base. Cut into slices and arrange in a salad bowl. • Peel and thinly slice the apples, coarsely chop the walnuts and cut the cheese into small dice. • Drain the raisins and add to the salad bowl along with the apples, nuts and cheese. • Use a separate bowl to prepare a vinaigrette dressing with the mustard, sherry vinegar and oil (½ groundnut, ½ walnut). • Season the dressing, pour over the contents of the salad bowl and mix carefully.

✚ Try replacing the apples with kiwi fruit – they work just as well.

Chicory tart Tatin with goat's cheese

> 8 chicory heads > 1/2 teaspoon grated orange rind > juice of 3 oranges > 1 tablespoon coriander seeds (crushed) > 1 goat's cheese 'log' > 1 batch shortcrust pastry (see recipe p. 146) <

• Preheat the oven to 180°C (350°F), gas mark 4. • Rinse the chicory and remove the bitter conical base. Cut in half and arrange in a flan dish. • Add the orange zest and juice and crushed coriander seeds. • Cover with kitchen foil so that the foil is touching the liquid. • Cook in the preheated oven for 35 minutes or until all the liquid has been absorbed. • While the chicory is cooking, cut the goat's cheese 'log' into slices and, when the dish

Hot tip

Use uncooked chicory leaves to make 'chicory boats' for an appetizer that is both attractive and nutritious (*see recipe p. 111*).

oven, arrange the slices of cheese on the endive. •
Roll out and cover with the pastry, tucking it well into
the inside edge of the dish to seal the contents. Cut a
small cross in the center of the pastry with a knife. •
Return to the oven for 20 minutes and then turn out
upside-down onto a serving dish.

✚ This endive tart tatin can be served as a first
course or as a main course with a green salad.

Cream of endive soup

> 4 endive heads > 2 oz butter > 2 chicken
bouillon cubes, dissolved in 4 cups hot water >
²/₃ cup light cream > walnut bread, to serve <

• Rinse the endive, remove the bitter conical base
and cut into slices. • Melt the butter in a large pan
and let the endive sweat for 5 minutes. • Add the
chicken bouillon and simmer over a low heat for 10
minutes. • Blend in an electric blender, add the light
cream and then blend again to enhance the soup's
creamy texture.

✚ Serve with toasted walnut bread—the flavors
go really well together.

Endive boats

> 1 endive head > 5 oz blue cheese > 2 oz
butter > 1 teaspoon cognac > pine nuts <

• Rinse the endive, drain well and remove the bitter
conical base. • Remove the leaves one at a time. •
Use a fork to mash the blue cheese and butter in a
bowl and add the cognac. • Lightly toast the pine nuts
by dry-frying. • Fill the endive leaf "boats" with the
cheese mixture and sprinkle with pine nuts.

✚ You can use variuos fillings, for example, cream
cheese and cumin, cream cheese and salmon roe.

Braised endive with honey and orange

> 4 endive heads > 2 knobs of butter > 2 tablespoons
clear honey > juice of 1 orange (or 2 tablespoons
lemon juice <

• Rinse the endive, remove the bitter conical base and
cut into slices. • Melt the butter in a pan and brown the
endive for 5 minutes. • Add the honey and orange (or
lemon) juice and cook until the liquid caramelizes.

✚ Serve as an accompaniment for pork chops
or chicken suprême.

This root vegetable is closely related to the cabbage and mustard plants. In ancient times, it grew wild in northern Europe and was a great favorite with the Romans. Today, turnips are less popular and, sad to say, are rarely eaten as a vegetable in their own right but tend to be used in stews and vegetable soups. However, their qualities—quick and easy to prepare, low in calories, extremely nutritious (a major plus in winter)—make a good case for their reinstatement as a cooked or raw vegetable.

Turnips,
a user's guide

Hardy winter varieties
Round purple-top variety
Spring varieties, sometimes sold with their leaves

Hardy winter varieties: These round or top-shaped turnips with white or yellow flesh are of excellent quality and store well. They are sometimes sold with their leaves which, combined with a bunch of watercress, can be used to make a nourishing green soup (*see page 134*, Cream of watercress soup).

Round purple-top variety: (Purple-Top White Globe), has a more subtle flavor than the white or yellow varieties but is less hardy (it freezes if the temperature drops too low).

Spring varieties: Sold at the end of winter. These tender young turnips (which can be flat, cylindrical or globular) have a mild flavor and are ideal for using raw or grated. Try them sliced with crème fraîche, diced apple and lemon juice.

> **Choosing for quality**
Choose firm, smooth turnips with unblemished skins.
Ideal size: As small as possible.
Bad signs: If they are too light, turnips may be hollow and stringy, especially towards the end of the season.

> **Storage**
Turnips keep well for several days in the refrigerator or in a cool place. If they are sold with their leaves, leave them on.

> **Preparation**
Washing Young turnips should be washed carefully—there's no need to peel them.
Peeling Older turnips need to be peeled if the skin is too tough, in which case there's no need to pre-wash.
Handy hint When boiling turnips, a crust or chunk of bread in the water prevents unpleasant cooking odors.

Calendar

Energy
20 kcal per 100 g

Nutritional advantages
Rich in sulfur (good for the skin), potassium and sugar. Turnips also contain large amounts of Vitamin C, calcium, and iodine.

Turnips—especially spring varieties—can be eaten raw, grated like carrots and seasoned with a French dressing (vinaigrette). Blanching tempers their rather strong flavor, while cooked turnips are delicious in sweet-and-sour dishes.

Turnips, simplicity itself

Honey-glazed turnips

> 2 lb turnips > butter for cooking > 2 tablespoons clear honey (Demerara sugar or maple syrup can be used instead) > coriander seeds (optional) <

• Rinse and peel the turnips, and cut into halves or quarters, depending on their size. • Melt a generous knob of butter in a pan and brown the turnips, turning and shaking the pan to make sure they are coated with the butter. • Add the honey, sugar or syrup and cover with water. • Cover and leave to cook for 30 minutes, until the water has evaporated.

➕ Try adding a teaspoon of crushed coriander seeds at the same time as the honey. Serve with duck, pork or pan-fried foie gras.

Turnip "sauerkraut"

> 2 turnips > 1 tablespoon goose fat, or butter > 5 juniper berries, lightly crushed > ¾ cup white wine > salt and freshly ground black pepper <

• Peel the turnips, and cut into very thin strips, rather like sauerkraut. • Melt the goose fat or butter in a high-sided skillet or wok and brown the strips of turnip. • Add the crushed juniper berries and wine. • Season to taste with salt and pepper, cover and cook for 10 minutes.

➕ This is delicious served with poached, lightly smoked pork sausage, boiled potatoes, and mustard.

Turnip tart Tatin

> 2 lb turnips > 4 oz butter > 4 oz sugar > 1 batch plain pastry (*see page 146*) > salt and pepper <

• Preheat the oven to 350°F. • Peel and slice the turnips, and cook for 5 minutes in boiling salted water. • Melt the butter and sugar in an flameproof, non-stick pie pan and caramelize to a rich, dark brown color. Remove from the heat. • Arrange layers of turnips in concentric circles in the pan, taking care not to burn yourself—the pan will be hot! • Roll out and cover with the pastry, tucking well in to seal the filling. • Cut a cross in the pastry with the tip of a knife and cook in the preheated oven for 20 minutes. • Let stand for a few minutes then turn the tart out upside-down onto a serving plate.

➕ This turnip tart Tatin is delicious served with sliced breast of duck or goose.

Turnips and prunes au gratin

> 2 lb turnips > ½–¾ cup pitted prunes > 2 oz butter > 1 cup thick crème fraîche, or whole-milk yogurt > 2 egg yolks > salt and freshly ground black pepper <

• Preheat the oven to 350°F. • Peel and slice the turnips. • Chop the prunes. • Melt the butter in a skillet and brown the turnips to a soft, melting texture. Season and add the prunes. • Turn the mixture into a gratin dish. • Beat the crème fraîche in a bowl, add the egg yolks and spread the mixture over the turnips and prunes. • Cook in the preheated oven for 5 minutes, until the top is golden brown.

➕ A simple yet stylish accompaniment for roast duck or lamb.

Hot tip

Small turnips glazed with maple syrup—as well as sweetening the turnips, the syrup also adds its distinctive herbaceous flavor.

Turnips with a sweet-and-sour dressing

> 4 turnips > sherry vinegar > groundnut oil >
3 tablespoons clear honey > salt and freshly ground
black pepper <

• Peel the turnips and slice thinly. • Plunge into boiling
unsalted water for 20 seconds, then rinse with cold
water. • Drain on paper towels and place in a salad
bowl. • In a separate bowl, make a vinaigrette with the
sherry vinegar, and groundnut oil, season to taste and
add the honey. • Sprinkle the sweet-and-sour dressing
over the turnips.

✚ This dish makes an unusual vegetable
accompaniment to various meats.

Glazed turnips and radishes

> 1 lb small turnips > 1 bunch pink radishes >
4 oz butter > 4 oz sugar > 3 tablespoons vinegar >
salt and freshly ground black pepper <

• Rinse and trim the turnips and radishes. • Melt the
butter in a large, high-sided skillet and brown the
vegetables over a low heat. • Add the sugar and
vinegar. • Season and cook over a low heat, gently
turning the vegetables from time to time until they are
cooked through and glazed.

✚ A delicious and colorful accompaniment—ideal
for roast meat.

Turnip purée

> 1 lb turnips > 1 large potato > ²/₃ cup crème
fraîche, or whole-milk yogurt > ²/₃ cup milk >
2 oz butter > salt <

• Peel the turnips, and cut into halves or quarters,
depending on their size. • Peel the potato and cut

into pieces. • Plunge the turnip and potato pieces
into a large pan of boiling salted water and cook for
20 minutes or until tender. • Drain and mash thoroughly
with a potato masher, then turn the purée into a serving
dish. • Bring the crème fraîche and milk to a boil and
pour over the purée. • Add the butter and mix well.

✚ This tasty purée is delicious served as an
accompaniment to grilled fish.

The potato was introduced into Europe some 500 years ago, when the Indians of the Andes (its land of origin) were already selecting this tuber with the skill and expertise born of long practice. Since the 19th century, the potato has been the subject of scientific interest and the product of the very latest technology. Today, potatoes come in all shapes and sizes (round, oval, kidney-shaped or as fingerlings), colors (yellow, white, red) and textures (floury or waxy). Early varieties provide "new" potatoes that can be lifted and enjoyed in summer, while maincrops can be stored and eaten throughout the winter.

Potatoes,
a user's guide

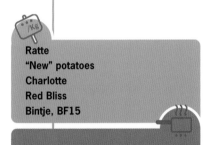

Ratte
"New" potatoes
Charlotte
Red Bliss
Bintje, BF15

Ratte: Excellent in purées and cooked in their skins.

"New" or "early" potatoes: This is a term for immature potatoes harvested in the spring or early summer. They are small and tender; don't need peeling, don't take long to cook and are at their best sautéed or steam-cooked, often served with a knob of butter and chopped mint or chives.

Charlotte: Yellow-skinned and yellow-fleshed, a good all-round potato, suitable for mashing and roasting.

Red Bliss: The classic American, red-skinned potato. Makes an idea salad potato and gives a lovely tender "new potato" if you want to steal some of your home-grown ones ahead of the game.

Bintje, BF15: Originally from Holland these large, yellow-fleshed potatoes are becoming popular, far from their homeland, because of their versatility.

> **Choosing for quality**
Choose firm, unblemished potatoes with no spade marks and no signs of damp or mold.
Ideal size: Potatoes of the same size will have the same cooking time.
Bad signs: If potatoes begin to sprout, discard them, as the shoots are toxic.

> **Storage**
Maincrop potatoes keep for months in a cool place but early varieties are fragile and only keep for about 5 days.

> **Preparation**
Washing or peeling Early varieties can simply be scrubbed under running water, maincrop potatoes have to be peeled. If they have to be put to one side after peeling, always keep them in cold water.
Handy hint Potatoes absorb salt, so don't use too much when cooking. They can also be used to 'rescue' an over-salted dish. If this happens, simply reheat the dish adding two potatoes, cut into pieces. Remove the potatoes when they've had time to absorb the salt and the dish will be much improved. Clever, or what?

Calendar

Energy
85 kcal per 100 g
(when boiled)

Nutritional advantages
Rich in vitamins B and C, with high magnesium content.

Potatoes are a universal vegetable that go well with anything—with country fare or haute cuisine, meat or seafood, butter, cream, or olive oil. But a light sprinkling of sea salt may be all they need.

Potatoes, simplicity itself

Butter-glazed new potatoes

> 2 lb small new potatoes > 1 lb slightly salted butter > pepper <

• Rinse but do not peel the potatoes and leave to cook in the melted butter over a low heat, for 20–25 minutes. • Drain, season with pepper and serve immediately.

✚ The ultimate basic potato recipe, but not so good for the waistline!

Plain potato purée

> 2 lb potatoes > ¾ cup milk > 4 oz butter > salt <

• Peel the potatoes, cut into same-sized pieces and cook in a little salted water for 20 minutes. • While the potatoes are cooking, heat the milk in a small pan. • Drain the potatoes and mash with a potato masher (never use a food processor). • Add the warm milk and butter and mix well—mix from top to bottom, rather than stirring, as this will make the purée runny. If necessary, cover the purée and reheat in the microwave.

You can flavor a potato purée in a number of different ways:

– olive oil: replace half the butter with extra-virgin olive oil;

– olives: add 20 (pitted and chopped) black olives;

– horseradish: add 1 tablespoon of grated horseradish or creamed horseradish for a milder flavor;

– coarse-grain mustard: add 2 tablespoons coarse-grain mustard;

– saffron: add 2 pinches of saffron threads diluted in 3 teaspoons of warm, light cream;

– cumin: add 1 tablespoon ground cumin, the juice of 1 lemon, and replace half the butter with extra-virgin olive oil;

– truffles: add a few shavings of preserved truffles, a little truffle oil or, better still, small pieces of fresh truffle.

✚ You can also flavor potato purée by adding another cooked vegetable, such as celery, carrots, artichoke hearts, pumpkin, varying the proportions (⅔ or ⅓) to taste

Potato pancakes

> 1 lb meal potatoes > 2 eggs > ⅔ cup all-purpose flour > oil for cooking > salt and freshly ground black pepper <

• Peel, wash and dry the potatoes, and then grate using a medium-sized grater. • Beat the eggs in a mixing bowl, add two-thirds of the flour, and season with salt and pepper. • Add the grated potato and mix well. • Shape the mixture into small pancakes and coat each side with the rest of the flour. • Fry until golden brown in a lightly oiled non-stick skillet.

✚ Vary the recipe by adding 4–5 bacon strips, dry-fried into "matchsticks," to the pancake mixture.

Potatoes baked in kitchen foil

> Use medium to large potatoes, sold especially for baking > butter, sea salt, sour cream, chopped chives, to serve <

Hot tip

Encourage your favorite supermarket to stock unusual varieties and/or seasonal potatoes by buying them to try yourself, or watch out for them in farmer's markets and specialist vegetable store.

• Preheat the oven to 350°F. • Rinse and dry the potatoes, and wrap individually in kitchen foil. • Place on a baking tray and cook in the preheated oven for about 1 hour.

✚ When your guests open their foil parcels, they can cut their potato, season it with a little sea salt, and add a knob of butter or a spoonful of sour cream sprinkled with chopped chives. This is such a simple and delicious way to prepare potatoes.

Gratin dauphinois

> 2 lb potatoes > 1³⁄₄ cups milk > 1 cup light cream > 2 eggs > 1 garlic clove (peeled) > pinch of grated nutmeg > 2 oz butter > salt and freshly ground black pepper <

• Preheat the oven to 325°F. • Peel and thinly slice the potatoes. • Heat the milk and cream together. • Beat the eggs in a large mixing bowl and add the warm milk and cream. • Season with salt and pepper, and add the nutmeg. • Rub the inside of a gratin or shallow ovenproof dish with the garlic clove and then grease generously with butter. Cover the base of the dish with a layer of half the potato slices and pour over half the egg mixture. Add another layer using the rest of the potatoes and cover with the rest of the egg mixture. • Dot with knobs of butter and cook in the preheated oven for 1 hour or until cooked through and golden on top.

✚ Cover the gratin with kitchen foil if it starts to brown too quickly.

-20 Salmon "sushi"

> 2 lb potatoes > fresh chives with long stems > smoked salmon > cherry tomatoes (or salmon roe, or thick crème fraîche or sour cream) > salt <

• Peel the potatoes, cut into chunks and cook for 20 minutes in a small quantity of very slightly salted water. • Plunge the chives (using the same number of stems as there are potato chunks) into the water for 30 seconds and then drain the potatoes and chives. • Allow to cool. • Cut thin slices of smoked salmon to the same size as the potato chunks. • Wrap a slice of salmon around each piece of potato and tie with a softened chive stem. • Top with half a cherry tomato, or a spoonful of salmon roe or thick crème fraîche.

✚ The "sushi" can be prepared in advance, covered with plastic wrap and kept in the refrigerator.

-20 Potato "blinis"

> 1 lb potatoes > 2 eggs > 3 tablespoons light cream > scant ¹⁄₂ cup all-purpose flour, sifted > light vegetable oil for cooking > salt <

• Peel the potatoes, cut into equal-sized pieces and cook for 20 minutes in a small quantity of boiling salted water. • Drain and mash the potato pieces with a potato masher (never use a food processor) and turn into a large mixing bowl. • Add the eggs, light cream, and sifted flour, and mix well. • Heat the oil in a large non-stick skillet. • Ladle small amounts of the mixture into the pan, making sure they are spaced well apart, flatten gently and cook for 2 minutes on each side.

✚ Serve these small savory pancakes with cold ham, broiled bacon or smoked salmon and a small spoonful of thick crème fraîche or sour cream.

comeback

Some vegetables go out of style as others gain in popularity. Today, some of these "unfashionable" vegetables are making a comeback. They are mainly hardy plants, which means they can be grown without the use of chemicals, and their revival coincides with the interest in organic foods. They also offer a wider variety of flavors since, while our forebears had a hundred or so different types of vegetables at their disposal, today we make do with less than thirty!

Chinese artichokes and rutabaga, a user's guide

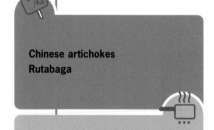

Chinese artichokes
Rutabaga

Chinese artichokes: are small, convoluted and indented tubers that originated in Japan. They are relatively rare, but watch out for them in specialist vegetable stores and markets. Their delicate, subtle flavor is reminiscent of artichokes, or salsify, and are popular for their crisp, crunchy texture, whether eaten raw or cooked, pan-fried or braised.

Rutabaga: was once used exclusively for animal fodder. It has a sweet yet spicy flavor and is best steamed to preserve its texture. It is also delicious well mashed with butter and pepper and is one of the key elements of the traditional Scottish dish of haggis with "bashed neeps and champit tatties."

Chinese artichokes

> **Choosing for quality**
Choose only firm tubers with iridescent white flesh.
Ideal size: None.
Bad signs: Soft, beige-colored tubers are past their best.

> **Storage**
Keep in the refrigerator, in a plastic bag, and they will remain firm and crunchy for up to 3 days.

> **Preparation**
Washing and drying Chinese artichokes require very little preparation. Wash and then rub dry with a cloth to remove the outer layer of skin.

Rutabaga

> **Choosing for quality**
Choose the heaviest and densest rutabaga for its size.
Ideal size: Medium, avoid large rutabaga as these can be stringy.
Bad signs: If they are too light, rutabaga may be hollow or, worse still, worm-eaten.

> **Storage**
Rutabaga keeps well for over a month in the refrigerator.

> **Preparation**
Peel with a paring knife.

Calendar

Energy
Rutabaga: 34 kcal per 100 g
Chinese artichokes: 80 kcal per 100 g

Nutritional advantages
Rutabaga is rich in Vitamin C.

Cardoons and Jerusalem artichokes, a user's guide

Cardoons

> **Choosing for quality**

Make sure the leaves have a good, green color and are unblemished.

Ideal size: They should be fairly big.

Bad signs: If the stems are green, don't buy them—they should be nice and white.

> **Storage**

Keep in the refrigerator for up to 3–4 days.

> **Preparation**

Washing and removing the strings Wash the stems and cut into pieces a few inches long, removing the strings that run through the stems (rather like stringy celery).

Jerusalem artichokes

> **Choosing for quality**

The artichokes should be as smooth and regular as possible, to make peeling easier.

Ideal size: As large as possible, for the same reason.

Bad signs: If they are soft or flaccid, the artichokes are too old.

> **Storage**

Jerusalem artichokes keep well in the refrigerator, in a plastic bag.

> **Preparation**

Cleaning and peeling The skin of the Jerusalem artichoke is thin and nutritious and it is not necessary to peel them unless desired, especially if newly lifted from the earth. A good scrub under running water should be all that is necessary. When cut or peeled, keep in water, or it will quickly discolor.

Cardoons
Jerusalem artichokes

Cardoon: Although it resembles an artichoke, it is the stems of a cardoon that are eaten, not the head. Like the artichoke, it belongs to the thistle family from whose Latin name, *Carduus*, its name derives. Not now a commonly found vegetable, it takes time, trouble and a fair amount of space to grow. Look out for it in season in farmer's markets or specialist vegetable store. The stems are usually boiled and prepared au gratin, in a sauce or simply served with a knob of butter.

Jerusalem artichoke: This amazingly productive plant (also known as "sunchoke") is becoming more widely available. It has an extremely subtle and interesting flavor and is prepared like a potato, although peeling is not always necessary. Its name is nothing to do with the Middle East—it derives from the Italian *girasole* ("sun follower") and indicates its relationship to the sunflower.

Calendar

Energy

Cardoons: 33 kcal per 100 g
Jerusalem artichokes: 78 kcal per 100 g

Nutritional advantages

Cardoons: Contain potassium, calcium, magnesium and small amounts of protein.

Jerusalem artichokes: Are rich in fiber and potassium, as well as iron, phosphorous, copper and magnesium.

These neglected vegetables go well together and can be used to create a delicious "old-fashioned" accompaniment. They can also be combined with chestnuts, artichoke hearts, and mushrooms.

Comeback vegetables, simplicity itself

 ### Braised Chinese artichokes

> 2 lb Chinese artichokes > 1 oz butter > 4 fresh parsley sprigs or chive stems, chopped > salt and freshly ground black pepper <

• Wash and drain the artichokes, and brown in the butter in a high-sided pan or Dutch oven. • Add ½ cup water, cover and cook for 10 minutes, stirring occasionally (the artichokes should remain slightly firm). • Season to taste and add the chopped herbs.

✛ The flavor of the artichokes makes a perfect complement for thickly sliced ham or veal escalopes in a cream sauce.

 ### Jerusalem artichokes and mushrooms au gratin

> 8 Jerusalem artichokes > 2 oz butter > 4 large mushrooms > generous cup freshly grated Gruyère cheese <

• Preheat the oven to 350°F. • Scrub (or peel) and slice the artichokes—the slices should be about ¼-inch thick. • Melt half of the butter in a skillet, brown the artichokes for 10 minutes, then arrange in a gratin or shallow ovenproof dish. • Wipe and thinly slice the mushrooms. • Brown in the rest of the butter, in the same pan used for the artichokes, until the cooking juices have evaporated. • Add the mushrooms to the gratin dish, sprinkle with the grated cheese, and cook in the preheated oven for 20 minutes or until the topping is crisp and golden.

✛ Serve as an accompaniment for roast beef, pork or veal.

Cream of Jerusalem artichoke soup

> 4 large Jerusalem artichokes > 1 onion > 1 oz butter > 2 chicken bouillon cubes, dissolved in 4 cups boiling water > 1 cup light cream > salt and freshly ground black pepper (if required) <

• Peel the artichokes and the onion, and cut into quarters. • Melt the butter in a pan and brown the vegetables. • Add the chicken and cook over a low heat for 30 minutes. • Blend in an electric blender and add the light cream. • Season to taste with salt and pepper.

✛ Top with a few chopped, boiled chestnuts and a drizzle of walnut or hazelnut oil.

 ### Butter-glazed rutabaga

> 1 medium rutabaga > 1 oz butter > 1 tablespoon homemade chicken bouillon (rather than a bouillon cube) diluted in ¾ cup boiling water > granulated sugar > salt <

• Peel and dice the rutabaga. • Melt the butter in a pan and lightly brown the rutabaga with a pinch of salt and a pinch of sugar. • Add the chicken bouillon. • Bring to a boil, cover and cook for 10 minutes until the liquid has evaporated. • Take care it does not boil dry.

✛ You can replace the rutabaga in this recipe with turnips.

Hot tip

Jerusalem artichokes, when peeled, sliced and arranged around a chicken or joint of roasting meat, will absorb the meat juices. It's quick and easy to do and absolutely delicious.

Jerusalem artichokes sautéed in maple syrup

> 8 Jerusalem artichokes > 1 oz butter > 1 tablespoon maple syrup <

• Scrub, or peel, and slice the Jerusalem artichokes – the slices should be about $1/16$-inch thick. • Brown in a skillet with the butter. • Add the maple syrup and cook for 3 minutes—the artichokes should remain crunchy (al dente).

+ You can use clear honey instead of maple syrup. This is an original dish that makes a perfect accompaniment for calf's liver or pan-fried foie gras.

Cardoons in béchamel sauce

> 2 lb cardoons > 4 oz butter > 4 oz all-purpose flour > 4 cups milk > salt and freshly ground black pepper <

• Rinse the cardoons and cut into $1^{1}/4$-inch pieces, removing the strings. • Plunge into boiling salted water for 10 minutes. Drain, then turn into a serving dish. • Prepare the sauce by melting the butter in pan over a low heat, stirring in the flour and then the milk. • Bring to a boil and cook for 10 minutes, stirring continuously. • Season to taste and pour over the cardoons.

+ Alternatively, pour the mixture into a gratin dish, sprinkle with grated cheese and place under a preheated broiler until the topping is crisp and golden.

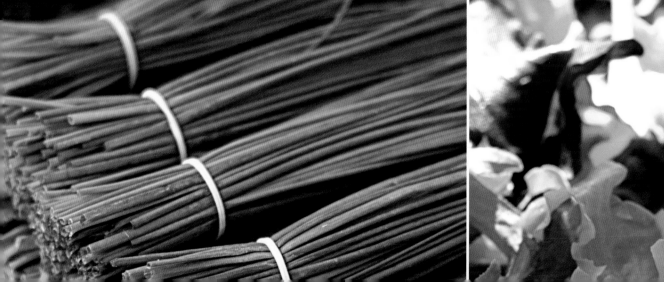

alliums

SALAD GREENS AND HERBS

Garlic, onion, and shallots are all liliaceous plants belonging to the genus Allium (from the Latin meaning "garlic"). Garlic is an ancient plant from the steppes of central Asia, renowned for its many medicinal properties. It contains essential oil whose principal allyl-based components combine with sulfur to give it its pungent flavor. These components are also found in an extremely volatile form in the onion.

Garlic, onions, and shallots, a user's guide

Garlic

Yellow, white and red onions; salad onions (sold with their stems); scallions

"Gray" shallots, round red shallots, elongated (the French "longue') shallots

Garlic: It should be used sparingly and its flavor should not dominate the dish; often a wipe round the inside of the serving dish with the cut side of a garlic clove will suffice. When using milder vegetables (e.g. mushrooms), replace with raw shallots, added just before serving.

Yellow, white, and red onions, salad onions (sold with their stems), scallions and button (or pickling) onions: Onions add a melting texture, extra body, and a touch of sweetness to a wide range of dishes, sauces, and stocks. Yellow onions are always cooked, while white and red (summer) varieties can be used cooked or raw. Salad onions are usually eaten without peeling, while their stems can be used in mixed herbs. Scallions are small, fresh onions harvested before the bulb develops. Button (or pickling) onions can be used whole in stews and casseroles, or boiled and served in a sauce as an accompaniment.

> **Choosing for quality**
Garlic bulbs should be firm and dry, while onions and shallots should be smooth with dry, flaking skins.
Ideal size: None.
Bad signs: If bulbs are light, dried out, or hollow, the garlic is too old. The same applies to onions and shallots, which may also have traces of mold or new shoots.

> **Storage**
Garlic: Pink Lautrec garlic will keep for up to 6 months stored in a dry place at a temperature of 53–59°F, without damaging the bulbs. Other types of garlic will only keep for a month.
Onions and shallots: Bulb onions can be stored throughout the winter months, salad and scallions can be kept in the refrigerator for up to 1 week

> **Preparation**
Garlic:
Peeling Fresh garlic can be cooked in its skin, which seals in the flavor and gives the taste of garlic without its pungency. Raw garlic is best crushed in a garlic press to make the most of its flavor.
Removing the shoots After 2–3 months, you'll need to remove any shoots. To prevent your fingers smelling of garlic simply rub them on something made of stainless steel (e.g. a spatula or the blunt edge of a knife).

Onions and shallots:
Peeling without tears Onions have between 1 and 3 skins. Peeling onions under running water will stop you crying.
Cutting without tears Rinse the knife frequently so that the water absorbs the volatile allyl-based components. Alternatively, wear safety glasses or swimming goggles!
Cooking without over-browning Don't let onions and shallots over-brown— if you do, they'll have a bitter, unpleasant taste. Don't use a food processor to chop onions as they'll lose their moisture and become bitter.

Calendar	Energy	Nutritional advantages
Garlic: Onions and shallots: all year round	Garlic: 138 kcal per 100 g Onions and shallots: 46 and 75 kcal per 100 g	Garlic reduces cholesterol, is good for the respiratory tract and relieves hypertension. It also has diuretic, depurative, and antiseptic properties.

Garlic goes wonderfully with lamb, pork, chicken, mushrooms...and is an essential ingredient in the preparation of stocks, marinades, and sauces. However, it totally destroys asparagus and seafood. Onions, on the other hand, go with absolutely everything, while the subtlety of shallots can be used sparingly to complement the most delicate flavors.

Garlic, onions, and shallots, simplicity itself

-20 Garlic and cilantro soup with poached eggs

> 4 garlic cloves > 4 cups water > 1 bunch cilantro > 3–4 slices white sandwich bread > 4 eggs > vinegar for cooking > 2 tablespoons olive oil > salt and freshly ground black pepper <

• Peel and thinly slice the garlic cloves and place in a pan. • Add the measured water and bring to the boil. • Add a little salt and boil for 10 minutes. • Meanwhile, chop the cilantro, cut the bread into small cubes and poach the eggs in a pan of vinegar water. • Arrange the ingredients in soup bowls, pour on the garlic soup and drizzle with olive oil.

✛ A simple but original dish, which is quick to prepare.

Chicken with onion and lemon grass

> 4 large onions > 1–2 stems lemon grass > oil for cooking > 4 tablespoons soy sauce > 4 chicken breasts, cut into slices about 1/2 inch thick > 1 pinch mild chili powder <

• Peel and slice the onions and chop the lemon grass. • Lightly brown the onions and lemon grass together in a lightly oiled wok or skillet. • Mix in 2 tablespoons of the soy sauce, turn into a serving dish, set aside and keep warm. • Lightly brown the chicken slices in the wok or skillet, adding 1 tablespoon oil if required. • Add the rest of the soy sauce and the chili powder, and cook for 5 minutes. • Return the onions and lemon grass to the pan to warm through and then turn into the serving dish.

✛ Serve with a bowl of rice for an authentically Oriental flavor.

Pink garlic croquettes

> 3 heads pink Lautrec garlic > olive oil for cooking > 1 oz butter > 4–5 tablespoons all-purpose flour > 1 cup milk > 2 tablespoons grated Gruyère cheese > 5 egg yolks > breadcrumbs > oil for frying > salt and freshly ground black pepper <

• Separate and peel the garlic cloves and place in a pan. • Cover with olive oil and cook over a low heat for 25 minutes. • Drain the garlic and purée in a blender. • Prepare a Mornay sauce by melting the butter in a high-sided skillet and whisking in 3 tablespoons of the flour and the milk. • Add the grated cheese and season to taste. • Stir in the garlic purée and add the egg yolks. • Mix well and then shape the mixture into small balls about 1/2 oz each. • Roll the balls in the rest of the flour and the breadcrumbs and deep fry at 375°F or until a cube of bread browns in 30 seconds.

✛ A recipe from Parisian chef, Éric Frechon, who recommends serving these garlic croquettes with lamb chops and a green salad.

Garlic creams

> 2 heads garlic > 3/4 cup milk > 3/4 cup water > 1 egg, plus 1 egg yolk > 1 cup light cream > salt and pepper <

• Preheat the oven to 325°F. • Separate and peel the garlic cloves, remove any shoots, and place in a pan. • Cover with the milk and water and cook for 20 minutes. • Drain the garlic and blend to a smooth purée with a blender or garlic crusher. • Add the egg, egg yolk, and cream. Season to taste. • Pour the mixture into individual ramekin dishes and cook in a water bath (place in a roasting pan with hot water halfway up their sides) in the preheated oven for 30 minutes.

French onion soup

> 4 onions > butter for cooking > oil for cooking >
2 tablespoons flour > 4 cups chicken bouillon made
with a cube, or 4 cups water, if preferred > 1 slice
per serving of day-old French or farmhouse bread >
generous cup freshly grated Gruyère cheese> salt and
freshly ground black pepper <

• Peel and slice the onions. • Heat a mixture of butter
and oil in a Dutch oven or large pan, and lightly brown
the onions. • Sprinkle with the flour, cook for 3 minutes
and then add the chicken bouillon or water. • Season
with salt and pepper to taste and leave to simmer for
30 minutes. • Pour the soup into individual flameproof
serving bowls, top with the slices of bread and sprinkle
with the grated cheese. • Place under a preheated
broiler for around 10 minutes or until the cheese is
crusty and golden.

✛ Vary by adding a few slices of peeled tomato to
the bread slices before sprinkling with the Gruyère
cheese, or use a different cheese of your choice.

Onion compote

> 1 lb onions > $\frac{1}{2}$ chicken bouillon cube,
dissolved in $\frac{3}{4}$ cup hot water > 1 cup raisins > 1 oz
butter <

• Peel and slice the onions. • Cook for 25 minutes in
a pan with the chicken bouillon. • Drain the onions,
retaining the cooking juices, and purée until smooth
with an electric blender. • Soak the raisins in the
cooking juices. • Reheat the onions and raisins in a pan
with a large knob of butter and serve.

✛ Why not flavor the compote with a pinch
of cinnamon or curry powder, or a dash of
blackcurrant liqueur? Serve with fresh foie gras.

Flammenküche ("flame cake" from Alsace, France)

> 1 cup diced smoked bacon > 7 oz cream cheese
> $\frac{2}{3}$ cup crème fraîche, or thick yogurt > $1\frac{1}{2}$ table-
spoons all-purpose flour > 2 tablespoons light vegetable
oil > 2 pizza bases > 1 onion <

• Preheat the oven to 350°F. • Lightly brown the bacon
in a little oil and drain on paper towels. • In a bowl
mix the cream cheese, crème fraîche, flour, and oil. •
Spread the mixture on the pizza bases. • Peel and
slice the onion. • Arrange the onion and diced bacon on
the cheese mixture. • Cook in the preheated oven for
15 minutes.

Oven-baked garlic chicken

> $3\frac{1}{4}$ cups all-purpose flour > $10\frac{1}{2}$ oz sea salt
> 4 eggs > thyme flowers > 1 free-range chicken
($2\frac{1}{2}$–$3\frac{1}{2}$ lb) > 3 heads garlic > 4 thyme sprigs > olive
oil for cooking > salt and pepper <

• Preheat the oven to 475°F. • Mix the flour, sea salt,
eggs and thyme flowers to a dough with a little water. •
Let stand for 10 minutes. • Rinse, dry and season the
chicken cavity. • Roughly crush the garlic cloves and
place in the cavity along with the thyme sprigs. Tie the
legs together with kitchen string. • Heat some olive oil in
a skillet and brown the chicken. • Roll out the dough,
place the chicken in the center and carefully "wrap" the
chicken with the pastry, sealing the joins. • Cook in the
preheated oven for 45 minutes. Lower the temperature
to 400°F, and cook for a further 45 minutes. • Break
open the crust and test whether the chicken is cooked
through by piercing with a sharp skewer in the thickest
part. If the juices run clear the chicken is done.

✛ Brushing the pastry with egg yolk makes it
look more appetizing, but the pastry isn't
actually eaten.

The cultivated watercress we buy today is very different from that picked on the edge of streams in the past. For once, this is not such a bad thing since wild watercress is liable to be contaminated by parasites from drinking animals or agricultural chemicals leaching in from nearby fields. Today watercress is commercially grown in beds where it runs no risk of contamination while still retaining its delicious, peppery flavor. Watercress is extremely versatile and can be eaten raw in salads, cooked in soups, or as an accompaniment.

Watercress, a user's guide

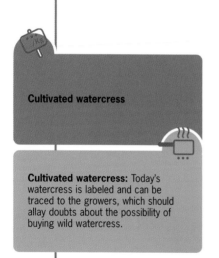

Cultivated watercress

Cultivated watercress: Today's watercress is labeled and can be traced to the growers, which should allay doubts about the possibility of buying wild watercress.

> **Choosing for quality**
Choose watercress with unblemished, uniform, green leaves.
Ideal size: None.
Bad signs: Don't buy watercress with withered, yellowing leaves.

> **Storage**
Don't expose watercress to air and light—it is grown in forcing beds. Wrap in a damp cloth and store in the vegetable compartment of the refrigerator—but don't keep it for more than 2 days.

> **Preparation**
Rinsing and picking over Watercress should never be soaked. Rinse under running water just before you use it. Pick over carefully and discard any unsightly leaves.
Removing the stems There's no need—every part of watercress can be used.

Calendar

Energy
40 kcal per 100 g

Nutritional advantages
Watercress is rich in Vitamin C, iron, calcium, and magnesium (which help prevent cardiovascular diseases).

Cooked or raw, the peppery flavor of watercress provides a perfect complement for fish and seafood. And what could be more delicious than watercress and goat's cheese, washed down with a glass of white wine?

Watercress, simplicity itself

Cream of watercress soup

> 1 bunch watercress > 2 oz butter
> 1 cup dry white wine > 2 chicken bouillon cubes, dissolved in 4 cups boiling water > 2 tablespoons short-grain rice > 1 cup light cream <

• Rinse and pick over the watercress. • Melt the butter in a pan and sweat the watercress for 3 minutes. • Add the white wine and bring to a boil. • Add the chicken bouillon and bring back t o a boil. • Add the rice, then simmer on a low heat for 25 minutes. • Blend in an electric blender until smooth, add the cream and blend again to give the soup its thick, creamy texture.

+ Warm and blend some of the cream and skim off the froth to create a cappuccino effect. Or for something a little more stylish, place a thinly sliced scallop in each bowl.

Watercress appetizers

> 1/2 bunch watercress > 2 square packages fresh Normandy demi-sel cheese, or 4 oz cream cheese > 1 teaspoon mustard > 5 slices white sliced bread > 20 shrimp <

• Rinse and pick over the watercress and dry with a salad spinner. • Chop finely in a blender and turn into a small mixing bowl. • Add your chosen cheese and the mustard and mix well. • Cut the sliced bread into bite-size triangles and spread with the cress mixture. • Place a peeled shrimp on each triangle.

+ For a variation, use pieces of smoked salmon instead of the prawns.

Watercress and broccoli creams

> 1 head broccoli > 1 bunch watercress > 1/2 cup light cream > 2 x 3 g gelatin leaves, or 1/2 sachet powdered > salt and freshly ground black pepper > cilantro leaves, to garnish <

• Discard the leaves and stem of the broccoli, and separate the florets. • Rinse and pick over the watercress. • Place the broccoli florets in a large pan of boiling salted water and cook for 7 minutes. • Plunge the watercress into the pan with the broccoli, bring back to a boil, and cook for a further 3 minutes. • Drain and mash the broccoli and watercress with a potato masher. • Warm the cream in a small pan and add the gelatin (in leaf form or powdered) as directed on the packet. • Add this mixture to the mashed vegetables, season, and pour into individual ramekin dishes. • Chill in the refrigerator for at least 2 hours before serving.

+ Serve the creams with a tomato coulis (or well-seasoned tomato juice) and garnished with cilantro leaves.

Watercress and mussel quiche

> 1 sheet plain pastry (*see recipe p. 146*)
> 2³/₄ pints mussels > ³/₄ cup dry white wine
> 1 bunch watercress > 3 eggs > ²/₃ cup light cream > ²/₃ cup milk > salt and freshly ground black pepper <

• Preheat the oven to 350°F. • Line a quiche dish with the pastry, prick the base and bake blind in the preheated oven for 5 minutes and then leave to cool. • Scrape and clean the mussels and open by cooking in a large pot with the wine. • Shake the pan and turn the mussels for 3 minutes. Remove

from the heat and drain, but retain the cooking liquid. • Shell the mussels, discarding any that have not opened. • Rinse and pick over the watercress and dry with a salad spinner or blot gently with paper towels. • Arrange in the precooked pastry case and add the shelled mussels. • Strain the cooking liquid into a bowl and mix together with the eggs, light cream, and milk. • Season and pour the mixture over the watercress and mussels. • Bake in the preheated oven for about 35 minutes.

✛ Serve the quiche with a watercress salad—well, why not?

Salmon and watercress parcels

> 1 bunch watercress > 1 unwaxed lemon > 4 thick slices salmon, about 5 oz each > oil for cooking <

• Preheat the oven to 350°F. • Rinse, pick over and drain the watercress, and slice the lemon. • Lightly oil 4 large pieces of waxed paper and place a slice of salmon on each one. • Place a small bunch of watercress and slice of lemon on each piece of salmon. • Wrap up the parcels and, if necessary, tie with kitchen string. • Cook on a baking sheet in the preheated oven for 10 minutes.

✛ You can spice up the parcels with slices of chorizo sausage, dry fried on each side for three minutes.

Watercress and haddock salad

> 1 bunch watercress > 2 shallots > 2 very fresh haddock fillets, skin removed > vinaigrette (see recipe p. 145) <

• Rinse and pick over the watercress and dry with a salad spinner, or blot gently with paper towels. • Place in a salad bowl. • Peel and chop the shallots and add to the watercress. • Rinse the haddock fillets and drain on paper towels. • Thinly slice the fish and add the slices to the salad bowl. • Make a vinaigrette using plenty of mustard, pour over the contents of the salad bowl and mix well.

✛ It is essential that the fish is very fresh for this recipe as it is eaten raw.

 ### Watercress pancakes with goat's cheese

> 1 bunch watercress > 8oz fresh goat's cheese > 2 eggs > grated rind of 1 lemon > $1/2$ cup pine nuts > 2 tablespoons olive oil > pinch of freshly grated nutmeg > 4 ready-made buckwheat pancakes (see below) > oil for cooking > salt and freshly ground black pepper <

• Preheat the oven to 350°F. • Rinse and pick over the watercress and dry with a salad spinner or blot gently with paper towels. • Mix the goat's cheese, eggs, lemon rind, pine nuts, and olive oil together in a bowl. Add the nutmeg, and season with salt and pepper. • Cut the buckwheat pancakes in half. • Arrange a little watercress on each pancake half and add a generous tablespoon of cheese mixture. Fold to form small triangles. • Use paper towels to oil a baking sheet and also brush the top of the pancake triangles with oil. • Place the triangles on a baking sheet and cook in the preheated oven for 15 minutes.

✛ Buckwheat pancakes are usually available from the "chilled" section of supermarkets.

Fresh herbs are an essential ingredient in good cuisine. You can make sure they are always within easy reach by growing them in a pot on the windowsill or keeping them in a glass in the refrigerator. Dill, chervil, cilantro, and tarragon all contain the same essential oil (which contains anethole) and can be used in combination or interchangeably. Other herbs such as chives, parsley, mint, basil, and sorrel (a culinary plant often regarded as a herb) have their own specific properties and must be used in their own right. Thyme, rosemary, savory, oregano, sage, and bay leaf can be used fresh or dried.

Herbs, a user's guide

Dill
Chervil
Cilantro
Tarragon
Chives
Parsley
Basil
Sorrel

Mint
Thyme
Bay leaf
Rosemary
Savory
Oregano
Sage

> **Choosing for quality**
Choose fresh herbs with a good, green color.
Ideal size: None.
Bad signs: If herbs begin to dry out or wilt, they are no longer fresh.

> **Storage**
Stand them in water, like flowers. Keep them in a glass or plastic beaker (much safer!) in the refrigerator.

> **Preparation**
Washing Rinse and dry with a cloth or paper towels before use.
Removing the leaves It's the leaves of herbs that are usually eaten but parsley, tarragon and cilantro stems can also be used to add flavor—simply discard after cooking.

Dill: Traditionally used to flavor fish, especially salmon.

Chervil: On a fried egg—it's simple and delicious.

Cilantro: For a flavor of Oriental and Asian cuisine.

Tarragon: Fresh and finely shredded, it is especially delicious in béarnaise and tartare sauces.

Chives: Use scissors to chop chives as finely as possible.

Parsley: Flat-leaf parsley has more flavor than the curly-leaf varieties.

Basil: Originally from India, basil is usually associated with Italy. It is the main ingredient in pesto.

Sorrel: Has a very distinctive flavor. It is used in omelets, soups, and sauces for fish.

Mint: Delicious in tea, sauces, tabbouleh, new potatoes, and with cucumber.

Thyme and bay leaf: Used with parsley in bouquet garni. Thyme is also used with parsley, sage, and marjoram in mixed herbs.

Rosemary: Used with thyme, sage, savory, and oregano, among other herbs, in herbes de Provence.

Savory: Goes well with pork.

Oregano: Closely related to marjoram. When dried it is wonderfully aromatic and works wonders with roast lamb and chicken.

Sage: Has more flavor dried than fresh. Dry by hanging in a corner of the kitchen. It is a natural partner for pork.

Calendar

Nutritional advantages
All herbs contain a number of vitamins (especially parsley), but you have to eat a lot for them to make a significant contribution to the recommended daily intake.

Herbs have an annoying tendency to dominate milder flavors, which can be both an asset and a disadvantage. You either have to use them in subtle and discreet combinations, or "go for it" and let them take pride of place.

Herbs, simplicity itself

-20 Quick sorrel soup

> 1 onion > 1 tablespoon butter > 1 chicken bouillon cube dissolved in 2 cups boiling water > 1 bunch sorrel > ¾ cup light cream > 1 cup freshly grated Gruyère cheese <

• Peel and thinly slice the onion. • Melt the butter in a pan and lightly brown the onion. Add the chicken bouillon and cook for 5 minutes. • Rinse, pick over and roughly chop the sorrel. • Put into an electric blender, add the hot bouillon and blend for 10 seconds. • Add the light cream and blend briefly to give the soup a light, frothy texture. • Pour into serving bowls and sprinkle with the Gruyère cheese.

✚ The sorrel can be replaced with a mixture of sorrel, lettuce and chervil.

Tabbouleh (made with bulgur wheat and flat-leaf parsley)

> 1 cup bulgur wheat > 1 onion > 3 sprigs flat-leaf parsley > 1 sprig mint > juice of 4 lemons > ½ cup olive oil > 4 tomatoes > salt and freshly ground black pepper <

• Prepare the tabbouleh day before you need it. • Soak the bulgur wheat in warm water in a mixing bowl, for 1 hour. • Drain through a strainer and leave to drain for 30 minutes to 1 hour. • While the wheat is draining, peel and thinly slice the onion; rinse and chop the parsley and mint. • Turn the drained bulgur wheat into a salad bowl and add the onion, herbs, lemon juice and olive oil. • Season to taste with salt and pepper and chill overnight in the refrigerator. • 1 hour before serving, dice the tomatoes and add to the tabbouleh. • Check the seasoning.

✚ Real tabbouleh contains lots of parsley; you can halve the amount of bulgur wheat.

-20 Marinated tuna with chive-and-chervil salad

> 4 thick slices fresh tuna > ¾ cup olive oil > 4 tablespoons lemon juice > 4 pinches mild chili powder > 1 bunch chives > 1 bunch chervil > 5–6 lettuce leaves > balsamic vinegar > sea salt <

• Rinse the tuna and dry with some paper towels. • Cut into large diced pieces and marinate for 30 minutes in ½ cup of the olive oil, the lemon juice, chili powder, and 4 pinches of sea salt. • While the tuna is marinating, rinse and shred the chives, and rinse the chervil and lettuce leaves. • Prepare a vinaigrette dressing with balsamic vinegar and the remaining olive oil. • Put the chives, chervil, and lettuce leaves in a small salad bowl, season with the vinaigrette and mix well. • Drain the tuna pieces and seal the flavor by frying or broiling for about 30 seconds over a high heat —the center should be raw with a melting texture.

✚ Half-cooked tuna is a real delicacy. If in doubt, it's better to undercook rather than overcook the tuna, as this would spoil everything.

Provençal mesclun (mixed herb salad)

> ¼ bunch each of chervil, parsley, cilantro and tarragon > 5–6 lettuce leaves > balsamic vinegar > well-flavored olive oil > salt and freshly ground black pepper <

• Rinse and finely shred all the herbs and place in a salad bowl. • Rinse, dry and add the lettuce

Hot tip

Chives—the more finely chopped they are, the more flavor they give, as more "oils" are released.

leaves to give volume. • Season with a vinaigrette made with balsamic vinegar and olive oil.

 Serve with potatoes cooked in their skins—simple but delicious. Why complicate matters?

 ### Aniseed-flavored herb cake

> $^1/_3$ bunch each chervil, dill, and tarragon >
1 tablespoon mustard > $2^2/_3$ cups all-purpose flour
> 1 x 7 g sachet dried yeast > 4 eggs > 9 tablespoons light vegetable oil > $^1/_2$ cup warm milk > 7–8 strips bacon, cut and dry-fried into "matchsticks" > $^1/_2$ cup freshly grated Gruyère cheese > salt and freshly ground black pepper <

• Preheat the oven to 350°F. • Rinse and finely shred the chervil, dill, and tarragon into a bowl. • In a small dish, mix $^1/_2$ teaspoon of salt and pepper with the mustard. • Mix together the flour, yeast, eggs, oil, warm milk, seasoned mustard, bacon "matchsticks", and grated cheese in a large bowl. • Add the shredded herbs to the mixture. • Pour the mixture into a greased cake tin lined with waxed paper. • Bake in the preheated oven for 45 minutes. • To test whether the cake is done, insert the blade of a knife into the center—it should come out clean.

 In spring, you can vary this recipe rather spectacularly by replacing half the flour with fresh peas—you'll certainly get a reaction!

Individual herb custards

> $^1/_4$ bunch each of chervil, parsley, cilantro, and tarragon > 2 eggs, plus 2 egg yolks > $^1/_2$ cup all-purpose flour > $^3/_4$ cup crème fraîche, or thick yogurt > $^3/_4$ cup milk > salt and freshly ground black pepper <

• Preheat the oven to 350°F. • Rinse and finely shred the chervil, parsley, cilantro, and tarragon into a bowl. • Beat the eggs and egg yolks together in a mixing bowl. • Add the flour, crème fraîche and milk. • Season and add the herbs. • Pour the mixture into individual ramekins and cook in the preheated oven in a water bath (place ramekins in a roasting pan filled with hot water half way up the ramekins) for 20–30 minutes.

 The custards should be firm to the touch. Serve with a green salad flavored with garlic.

There is a wide variety of salad greens available throughout the year. Field-grown salad greens are deliciously fresh and crunchy. Harvested during the day and transported overnight, they are on sale within 24 hours of being picked. This is certainly one luxury to be enjoyed on a daily basis.

Salad greens, a user's guide

Lettuce: Butterhead (round); Romaine; Crisphead (e.g. Iceberg)

Broad-leaved chicory

Arugula

Radicchio

Curly-leaf chicory (frisée)

Corn salad (lambs' tongues, mache)

Butterhead lettuce: Lettuce is so called due to its milky juice, from the Latin *lactuca*, from *lac* (milk). Field-grown butterheads, available May–Oct. are far superior to those grown under glass during the rest of the year.

Crisphead lettuce: The increasingly popular 'Iceberg' variety is in fact grown in California. Its food value is the same as other lettuces but it can keep for two weeks in its wrapping. Ideal for those who don't have time to buy fresh produce on a regular basis.

Curly-leaf chicory or frisée: With its finely divided frizzy leaves, is a native of south-east Asia. Field-grown chicory is available from May–Nov. The green leaves contain more vitamins and mineral salts than the yellow leaves in the center.

Broad-leaved chicory: Has a bitter, more distinctive taste than lettuce, similar to that of Belgian endive, its northern European cousin.

Radicchio: Crunchy and sharp tasting, these colorful red "lettuces" with white veins are not strictly a salad "green" but they work well in salads and can also be cooked. The Treviso variety is

> **Choosing for quality**
Choose crunchy salad greens with a moist center.
Ideal size: None.
Bad signs: A dry base means the salad greens were not picked just the day before.

> **Storage**
Salad greens have a high water content and dry out very quickly. They can only be kept for 1–2 days without being picked over. Once the greens have been picked over and dried with a salad spinner, store in an airtight box lined with a damp cloth or sealed in a plastic bag (this way they'll keep for 24–48 hours).

> **Preparation**
Washing Don't over-soak salad greens. If you do, they'll lose their vitamins and minerals.
Drying with a salad spinner or with paper towels This prevents the dressing being diluted.
Adding the dressing just before serving The vinaigrette 'cooks' the salad, which is why it has to be tossed at the last minute.
Handy hint Pour the vinaigrette into the salad bowl, cross the salad servers in the bowl and place the salad greens on the servers—this keeps them away from the vinaigrette.

long-leaved, similar to a Romaine lettuce, while the Chioggia variety is round and firm.

Corn salad (lambs' tongues, mache): The ultimate winter salad greens. Now sold ready to eat in trays or bags—ultra practical!

Arugula: This Mediterranean plant, also known as rocket, has become a household name. Serve with vinaigrette, with or without lemon, olive oil, and Parmesan, or in pasta sauces or pesto, where its strong, peppery taste makes it an effective alternative for basil.

Calendar

Energy
15 kcal per 100 g

Nutritional advantages
All salad greens are rich in vitamins C and E, as well as in trace elements, mineral salts and fiber.

Salads are delicious with fresh herbs (chives, chervil, parsley, tarragon), garlic, shallots, salad onion, scallions, and even certain flowers (borage, marigolds). Put them together and you have the Provençal mixed green salad known as mesclun.

Salad greens, simplicity itself

Radicchio in cream sauce

> 3–4 heads Chioggia radicchio (quantity depends on size) > 1¼ cups light cream > salt and freshly ground black pepper <

• Discard the bases of the radicchio and wash carefully. • Plunge into boiling salted water for 3 minutes. • Drain and rinse under the cold tap and then press between your hands to extract as much water as possible. • Put the radicchio in a high-sided skillet, pour on the cream, season with salt and pepper and cook for 30 minutes, until the cream has almost completely evaporated.

+ Serve the radicchio with roast veal, pork or poultry.

 ### Tortilla with arugula

> 10 oz arugula > 1 ball mozzarella cheese > 8 eggs > ½ cup freshly grated Gruyère cheese > oil for cooking > pinch of nutmeg > salt and freshly ground black pepper <

• Rinse and pick over the arugula and dry in a salad spinner or paper towels. • Cut the mozzarella into small cubes. • Beat the eggs in a bowl and add the diced Mozarella and grated Gruyère. • Season and add the nutmeg. • Heat some oil in a high-sided, nonstick skillet. • Pour in the egg mixture, add the arugula, then lower the heat, cover and cook for 5 minutes. • Turn the tortilla by placing a plate over the skillet and turning upside down so that the tortilla is on the plate. Return the tortilla to the pan and cook for a further 5–10 minutes.

+ You don't have to turn the tortilla—it will just be a little more runny. Serve as an appetizer, or as a main course with a arugula salad (why not?), or with slices of prosciutto.

 ### Corn salad with calf's liver, cherry tomatoes, and walnuts

> 7 oz corn salad > vinaigrette, using walnut oil (*see recipe p. 145*) > 1 calf's liver > oil for cooking > 1 tablespoon raspberry (or balsamic) vinegar > 8 cherry tomatoes (halved) > 10 walnuts > sea salt and freshly ground black pepper <

• Rinse and pick over the corn salad and dry with a salad spinner or paper towels. • Prepare a vinaigrette with the walnut oil. • Cut the calf's liver into thin strips—about ½ inch thick—and cook in an oiled skillet until the liver turns pink. Do not overcook! • Toss the salad with the vinaigrette in a salad bowl. • Season the liver with sea salt and pepper and arrange on the salad. • Deglaze the meat juices with the vinegar and pour over the salad. • Scatter over the cherry tomatoes and walnuts.

+ *Corn salad is extremely versatile:* try it with lentils and olives; beets and walnuts; pear and Dolcelatte cheese (or Gouda with cumin); foie gras and mango; warm potatoes and shallots; fillet of duck breast and pine nuts—the list is endless.

 ### Frisée with diced bacon and warm goat's cheese

> 10 oz curly chicory > vinaigrette, using a tasty olive oil (*see recipe p. 145*) > 2 cups diced bacon > 4 small, round goat's cheeses <

• Rinse, pick over and dry the frisée in a salad spinner or with paper towels. • Prepare a vinaigrette with the olive oil. • Dry-fry the diced bacon in a skillet and drain on paper towels. • Cut the goat's cheeses in half and brown

Hot tip

Hearts of small romaine lettuces, don't need picking over—they're all ready to eat!

142   Vegetables: at their freshest and best

under a preheated broiler. • Toss the frisée with the vinaigrette in a large salad bowl, scatter with the bacon bits and carefully arrange the goat's cheese halves on top.

✚ If you have any truffle oil or, better still, a few shavings of preserved, or even fresh, truffles, now is the time to use them—the combination is delicious. You can also use young dandelion leaves instead of curly chicory.

Cream of corn salad soup

> 7 oz corn salad > 1 oz butter > 2 large potatoes > 2 chicken bouillon cubes, dissolved in 4 cups boiling water (plain water can be used instead of bouillon cubes, if preferred) > 1 cup crème fraîche, or thick yogurt > salt and freshly ground black pepper <

• Rinse, pick over, and dry the corn salad in a salad spinner or with paper towels, then leave to sweat in a pan with the butter. • Peel and thickly slice the potatoes, and add to the pan. • Season with salt and pepper, add the chicken bouillon or water, and leave to cook for 20 minutes. • Blend the soup until smooth in an electric blender, add the crème fraîche and blend again to give it a thick, creamy texture.

✚ In this recipe, the corn salad works in much the same way as watercress (see Cream of watercress soup p. 134) and makes a subtly flavored and absolutely delicious soup.

appendices

Basic recipes

Vinaigrette

> 1 teaspoon salt > $^{1}/_{2}$ tablespoon strong mustard
> $^{1}/_{2}$ cup balsamic vinegar > $^{1}/_{2}$ cup sherry vinegar >
$1^{1}/_{4}$ cups groundnut oil > $1^{1}/_{4}$ cups olive oil > freshly
ground black pepper <

• Mix the ingredients in a bowl, in the following order:
salt, mustard, balsamic vinegar, sherry vinegar,
groundnut oil, olive oil, and finish with a few turns of
the pepper mill.

• Use 1 tablespoon of this vinaigrette per person.
Preparing a large quantity of vinaigrette in advance
saves you having to make a new batch for each salad.

✚ Keep the vinaigrette in a glass bottle or jar with
a lid and shake well before use.

Japanese-style vinaigrette

> 1 tablespoon soy sauce > juice of 1 lemon >
7 tablespoons sesame oil > 4 tablespoons olive oil <

• Mix the ingredients in a bowl, in the following order:
soy sauce, lemon juice, sesame oil and olive oil.

✚ Drizzle over cucumber or raw vegetables—it
makes a pleasant change and is really delicious.

Italian-style vinaigrette

> 1 teaspoon salt > $^{3}/_{4}$ cup balsamic vinegar
> $^{3}/_{4}$ cup sherry vinegar > $2^{1}/_{2}$ cups olive oil > freshly
ground black pepper <

• Mix the ingredients in a bowl, in the following order:
salt, balsamic vinegar, sherry vinegar, olive oil, and
finish with a few turns of the pepper mill.

✚ As for traditional French vinaigrette, keep in
a glass bottle or jar with a lid and shake well
before use.

Tuna dip

> 7 oz cream cheese (made from cow's or ewe's milk)
> 10 pitted black olives > 1 tin tuna (drained) > salt
and freshly ground black pepper <

• Blend the cream cheese, olives, and tuna in an
electric blender and season to taste.

✚ An ideal dip for small sticks of raw or steamed
vegetables.

Onion dip

> 7 oz cream cheese > 4 oz feta cheese > 2 small
salad onions > paprika > cumin > salt and freshly
ground black pepper <

• Mash the feta and finely chop the onions. • Mix the cream cheese, feta and onions together in a bowl. • Sprinkle with paprika and cumin, and season to taste.

✚ An ideal dip for raw vegetables, especially carrots, mushrooms, cherry tomatoes, celery and fennel.

Béchamel sauce

> 2 oz butter > 3 large tablespoons all-purpose flour > milk > grated Gruyère cheese (optional) > grated nutmeg > salt and freshly ground black pepper <

• Preheat the oven to 350°F. • Melt the butter in a pan over a low heat. • Mix in the flour with a hand-held whisk and then gradually add the cold milk, stirring continuously, until you have the right quantity and consistency. • Season and sprinkle with nutmeg to taste, and add the grated cheese, if using, to the desired quantity. • Pour the béchamel sauce over a shallow ovenproof dish of precooked vegetables (e.g. steamed sliced carrots or leeks stewed in butter) and bake in the preheated oven for 30 minutes.

✚ Success guaranteed! You can lighten the sauce by adding an equal quantity of crème fraîche.

Fried garlic

> garlic cloves > olive oil <

• Peel and finely slice the garlic cloves. • Pan fry in olive oil for a few minutes only. • Do not leave the pan unattended as the finely sliced garlic burns quickly.

Plain pastry for savory quiches and tarts Tatin

> 1¾ cups all-purpose flour, sifted > 4 oz butter (softened) > 1 egg > ½ cup cold water > pinch of salt <

• Rub the flour, salt, and butter into a coarse breadcrumb consistency in a mixing bowl. • Mix in the egg and gradually add enough of the measured water to bind the mixture into a dough. • Shape into a ball and leave to stand in the refrigerator for 1 hour. • Roll out the pastry on a lightly floured board and use to line a quiche dish or pie tin.

✚ For sweetened plain pastry, add 1 tablespoon granulated sugar to the mixture.

Savory crisp mixture

> 1 scant cup all-purpose flour > 4 oz butter, softened > 1¾ cups breadcrumbs > 1 cup freshly grated Parmesan cheese > ½ cup pine nuts > 2 tablespoons olive oil > salt and freshly ground black pepper <

• Preheat the oven to 400°F. • Put the flour, butter, breadcrumbs, Parmesan, pine nuts, and olive oil in a mixing bowl. • Mix the ingredients with your fingertips until you have a coarse crumbly mixture. • Season to taste. • Sprinkle the crumble mixture over 3 lb precooked vegetables that have been drained and arranged in a gratin or shallow ovenproof dish. • Cook in the preheated oven for 25 minutes.

✚ This crisp works particularly well with summer vegetables—tomatoes, zucchini, and eggplants—used individually or together.

Savory cake mixture

> 2½ cups all-purpose flour,sifted > 1 sachet dried yeast > 4 eggs > ⅔ cup olive oil > ⅔ cup sweet white wine > 1 tablespoon mustard > 7 oz bacon, cut into "matchsticks" and dry-fried > 1¼ cups freshly grated Gruyère cheese > ½ teaspoon salt and pepper mixture <

• Preheat the oven to 350°F. • Place all the ingredients in a large mixing bowl and mix well together. • Add 1 cup steamed and chopped vegetables (black and green pitted olives or fresh mixed herbs). • Pour the mixture into 2 cake tins lined with waxed paper and bake in the preheated oven for 50 minutes. • Test by inserting the blade of a knife into the center of the cake—it should come out clean.

✚ The amounts given will make two cakes. You can eat one cake and freeze the other—it makes an excellent snack or appetizer for those unexpected guests.

Quiche or gratin mixture

> 3 eggs > 3 tablespoons crème fraîche, or thick whole-milk yogurt > ¾ cup warm milk > ¾ cup freshly grated Gruyère cheese > salt and freshly ground black pepper <

• Preheat the oven to 325°F. • Mix the eggs, crème fraîche and warm milk together in a mixing bowl. • Season to taste and add the grated cheese. • Pour the mixture over 2 lb steamed vegetables arranged in a gratin dish or in a quiche dish lined with plain pastry. • Cook in the preheated oven for 40 minutes.

✚ Flavor the mixture with spices or herbs, depending on the vegetables used—cumin with carrots, chives with mushrooms, basil with zucchini…

Mayonnaise

> 1 egg yolk > 1 tablespoon strong mustard > ¾ cup grapeseed oil > 1 teaspoon white wine vinegar (optional) > 1 teaspoon salt > freshly ground black pepper <

• Stand a bowl on a tea towel to stabilize it and add the salt, a few turns of black pepper, the egg yolk, and mustard. • Beat with an electric hand-held whisk while gradually incorporating the grapeseed oil one drop at a time to begin with, until it starts to thicken when the oil can be added in larger amounts. • Add the wine vinegar to give the mayonnaise an added tang (optional).

✚ Grapeseed oil is the only oil that doesn't congeal in the refrigerator, which means you can keep any leftover mayo and re-use it. For a successful mayonnaise, it is essential that all the ingredients are at the same temperature. If it begins to separate, put another yolk in a separate bowl and whisk in the curdled mayonnaise drop by drop, when all is well again continue to add the remaining oil.

Whipped cream with mayo and chives

> ⅔ cup whipping cream > ingredients for mayonnaise > ½ bunch chives (chopped) <

• Pour the cream into a bowl placed inside a bowl of ice cubes, and whip the cold whipping cream until it forms stiff peaks. • In another bowl, make the equivalent amount of mayonnaise. • Carefully mix the whipped cream and mayonnaise together and then add the chives.

✚ An ultra-light dip for shrimp and all kinds of steamed vegetables.

BASIC RECIPES

Vegetables go really well together to create a visual as well as a gastronomic feast. So, why not combine different varieties for a riot of shapes and colors?

The best of mixed veg

Mixed steamed veg

> *For the vegetables (2 lb):* 7 oz carrots
> 7 oz turnips > 7 oz peas > 7 oz broccoli
> 7 oz snow peas
> *For the dressing:* chopped parsley and cilantro
> butter > crème fraîche or vinaigrette flavored
with curry powder > sea salt and freshly ground
black pepper <

• Rinse and peel the carrots and turnips, and cut into sticks about $1\frac{1}{2}$ inches long. • Shell the peas, separate the broccoli florets, and top and tail the snow peas. • Start by steaming the carrots, turnips, and peas for 10 minutes, then add the broccoli and snow peas and steam for a further 5 minutes. • Season to taste. You can vary the dish with different dressings.

✚ All these vegetables will taste good with butter, oil, or crème fraîche, full fat or fat reduced—whatever your preference and diet requirements.

Diet vegetable soup

> 3 leeks > 1 stalk celery > 1 onion > 3 carrots
> 2 turnips > 1 garlic clove > 6 cups water >
1 bouquet garni > salt and freshly ground black
pepper > chopped parsley, to garnish <

• Rinse or peel the vegetables (if appropriate). • Slice the leeks, celery, and onion; dice the carrots and turnips. • Crush the garlic clove. • Bring the measured water to a boil, plunge in the vegetables and add the bouquet garni. • Add a little seasoning of salt and pepper and leave to simmer over a low heat for 1 hour. • Adjust the seasoning to taste, and serve sprinkled with the parsley.

✚ An ideal soup for the day after a party or quite simply as part of a healthy diet.

Homemade chicken stock

> giblets from 3 chickens (wing tips, neck,
gizzard…) > 3 carrots > 3 leeks > 2 turnips
> 1 stalk celery > 1 onion > 1 garlic clove >
8 cups water > 1 bouquet garni > salt and freshly
ground black pepper <

• Ask your butcher for chicken giblets. • Rinse, peel (if appropriate) and slice the carrots, leeks, turnips, celery, and onion, and crush the garlic clove. • Bring the measured water to a boil, plunge in the vegetables and add the bouquet garni. • Season to taste and leave to simmer over a low heat for $1\frac{1}{2}$ hours.

✚ Strain the liquid into a bowl and allow to cool. Leave overnight in the refrigerator and the next day the solidified fat will be easy to remove. Freeze the stock in small quantities. It is much better than using bouillon cubes which, though a useful standby, are a poor substitute for homemade stock.

Vegetable terrine

> 2 lb after preparation (choose 3 of either
carrots, turnips, peas, French or pole beans,
snow peas) > 3 eggs > 7 oz cream cheese > salt
and freshly ground black pepper <

• Preheat the oven to 350°F. • Rinse, peel where appropriate, and roughly chop the 3 chosen vegetables. • Steam each of them separately for approximately 5–10 minutes, depending on type of vegetable and whether using a steamer, microwave or pressure cooker. • Mix the eggs and cheese together in a large mixing bowl, and season to taste. • Arrange alternate layers of each vegetable and cheese mixture in a nonstick cake pan (or lined with waxed paper). • Cook in the preheated oven for 45 minutes.

Stir-fried vegetables

14 oz meat (chicken, duck, beef, or pork) > 4 tablespoons Japanese soy sauce > 1 garlic clove > 1 small piece fresh ginger > vegetables (zucchini, carrots, beansprouts, mushrooms, broccoli, snow peas, onions) > sprigs of fresh herbs (cilantro, parsley) > oil for cooking <

• Slice the meat thinly and marinate in the soy sauce for 30 minutes. • Peel and chop the garlic clove and fresh ginger. • Heat a lightly oiled wok, soften the garlic and ginger, and then add the drained meat. • Stir-fry for a few minutes until the meat is cooked through. Remove from the wok when ready and keep warm. • Stir-fry the vegetables in the cooking juices from the meat. When they are cooked but still slightly crunchy, return the meat to the wok and reheat for 2 minutes. • Sprinkle with chopped herbs before serving.

+ Stir frying is a wonderfully simple and healthy way to eat vegetables, provided you cook the ingredients in the correct order: firm ones first, softer ones next. Preparing all the ingredients in advance makes it easier still, especially if you have guests.

Vegetable curry

> 1 garlic clove > 1 onion > 4 potatoes > 2 carrots > $\frac{1}{2}$ cauliflower > 1 eggplant > 2 zucchini > 4 tomatoes > olive oil for cooking > 2 tablespoons coriander seeds, lightly crushed > 1 teaspoon each curry powder, cumin, turmeric, and mild chili powder > $\frac{3}{4}$ cup water > salt and freshly ground black pepper <

• Peel and chop the garlic and onion. • Peel and slice the potatoes and carrots. • Rinse the cauliflower and separate the florets. • Rinse and dice the eggplant and zucchini. • Rinse and slice the tomatoes. • In a high-sided skillet, soften the garlic and onion in a little olive oil with the coriander seeds. • Add the curry powder, cumin, turmeric, and chili powder. • Season to taste, add the potatoes and carrots and cook for 10 minutes. • Add the cauliflower, eggplant, and zucchini and cook for a further 10 minutes. • Finally, add the tomatoes and measured water, cover and cook for 30 minutes.

+ Serve as an accompaniment for meat or fish, or even delicious on its own.

Beef and vegetable stew

Serves 8

> 3 lb stewing beef > 8 leeks > 6 turnips > 8 carrots > 1 onion stuck with cloves > 1 bouquet garni > 4 sticks celery > 8 potatoes > 8 chunks marrowbone > salt and freshly ground black pepper <

• Cut the beef into largish cubes and put into a large pan or Dutch oven, cover with cold water and bring to a boil, removing scum and impurities at regular intervals. • Season with salt and pepper, cover and leave to simmer gently over a low heat for $1\frac{1}{2}$ hours, checking regularly that the meat is not overcooking. • While the meat is cooking, prepare and cut the vegetables to the required size. • Separate the white part of the leeks from the green leaves, tying the latter together with kitchen string. • Add the turnips, carrots, onion, and bouquet garni to the pan and cook for a further 30 minutes. • Finally, add the white part of the leeks, the bundle of green leaves, the celery, and potatoes and cook for a further 45 minutes. • Ladle some of the bouillon into a pan and poach the chunks of marrowbone for 10 minutes. • Serve separately.

+ Serve the stew with sea salt, mustard, and horseradish.

Vegetable risotto

> 2 chicken bouillon cubes, dissolved in 5 cups boiling water or 5 cups heated, homemade chicken stock > 1 onion > 2 tablespoons olive oil > 8 oz vegetable garnish (mushrooms, small vegetables) > $2\frac{1}{2}$ cups risotto rice (e.g. Arborio or Carnaroli) > 1 cup freshly grated Parmesan cheese > 2 oz butter (optional) <

• Keep the chicken stock warm. • Peel and finely chop the onion and soften in the olive oil in a large, high-sided skillet or wok, together with the vegetable garnish. • Add the rice and cook until the grains are translucent. • Add the chicken bouillon, one ladle at a time, stirring continuously so that the rice gradually absorbs the bouillon. It is important to wait until each ladleful is absorbed before adding the next. • When all the bouillon is incorporated, add the Parmesan and knobs of butter (if using) to thicken the risotto.

+ If you decide to flavor the risotto with herbs (cilantro) or spices (saffron), add the flavoring with the last ladle of bouillon.

Salade Niçoise

> 4 tomatoes > ½ cucumber > 1 fennel bulb
> 4 mushrooms > 2 salad onions (with stems)
> 4 artichoke hearts preserved in oil > 1 x 6–7 oz
can tuna > 4 hard-cooked eggs > 1 handful pitted
black olives > vinaigrette dressing (*see recipe
p. 145*) <

• Rinse and chop the fresh vegetables neatly but
not too small, and arrange in a salad bowl. • Drain
and slice the artichoke hearts. • Drain and flake
the tuna, quarter the hard-cooked eggs. • Add to
the salad bowl together with the olives, and season
with vinaigrette.

✚ In theory, Salade Niçoise is made with raw
vegetables only, but there's nothing to stop
you adding any of the following: a few small
precooked new potatoes, French beans, a handful
of corn, or even a few small vegetables preserved
in olive oil.

Pork and vegetable stew

Serves 8

> 1 green cabbage > 1 onion > 3 leeks >
8 carrots > 6 turnips > 1 stalk celery > 8 potatoes
> 1 garlic clove > vegetable oil for cooking >
1 bouquet garni > 1¾ lb pork (upper shoulder,
cut into medium-size pieces) > 1 joint pork spare
rib > 14 oz smoked ham, uncooked > 1 lightly
smoked pork sausage > salt <

• Blanch the cabbage and cut into quarters,
then plunge into a pan of boiling salted water for
5 minutes. • Peel and slice the onion and leeks
and peel and roughly chop the carrots and turnips.
• Wash and slice the celery. • Peel the potatoes.
• Peel and crush the garlic. • Soften and lightly
brown the onion and leeks in a large pan or Dutch
oven in a little oil. • Add the turnips and carrots,
bouquet garni, crushed garlic, and celery. • Add
the meat (except the sausage) and cover with cold
water. Bring to a boil and leave to simmer over a
low heat for 45 minutes. • Add the cabbage and
cook for a further 15 minutes. • Add the sausage
(pricked several times with a fork) and potatoes
(either left whole or halved if largish) and cook for
a further 30 minutes.

✚ This recipe serves 8—it's not really worth
making a stew for 4 people. So why not invite
your friends or neighbors to share it with you?

Chilled summer soup

> 5 large tomatoes (skinned) > 1 cucumber >
1 onion > 1 red bell pepper > ½ head celery >
3 slices white bread, crusts removed (or the
equivalent in stale breadcrumbs) > ¾ cup olive oil
> 2 cups milk > 4 tablespoons tomato ketchup
> Tabasco > ice cubes and croutons, to serve >
salt and freshly ground black pepper <

• Cut the tomatoes into eight and seed. • Peel
and dice the cucumber and onion. • Cut the bell
pepper and celery into small pieces. • Tear bread
slices into pieces and place with the vegetables
in a large bowl. • Add the olive oil, milk, ketchup,
and a few drops of Tabasco. • Mix well and season
to taste. • Cover with plastic wrap and leave to
marinate in the refrigerator for at least 2 hours—
it can be left for up to 2 days. • Blend the soup in
an electric blender and serve with a few ice cubes
and croutons.

✚ This recipe is based on gazpacho, an
uncooked soup from Andalucia—the
marinating replaces the cooking process. Serve
in glasses and add a few shrimp and thin slices
of avocado for a more stylish first course.

✚ Don't forget—this selection of "best of mixed
veg" recipes is not exhaustive—there's an
endless variety of all kinds of delicious soups and
vegetable dishes "out there"—be adventurous!

Best cooking methods

When it comes to vegetables, some cooking methods are better than others. The following guidelines should prevent any major blunders and help you make the most of your vegetables.

> **Boiling:** simply plunge the vegetables into boiling salted water, and test by trying them. Plunge green vegetables into iced water immediately after cooking to fix their lovely green color.

> **Steaming:** Place the vegetables in the basket of a pressure cooker or a wicker (or bamboo) steamer. Alternatively, cook them in a tightly covered casserole or a Dutch oven with very little liquid. These are the best methods for preserving the nutritional value of vegetables—the vitamins are not dissolved in water and there's no added fat.

> **Pressure cooking:** The ultimate fast-cooking method. The main disadvantage is that it's difficult to control the level of cooking and vegetables are sometimes overcooked. Not recommended if you like your vegetables slightly crunchy.

> **Braising or casseroling:** In a lightly oiled or greased casserole or covered pan, over a low heat. The vegetables often taste better than when cooked with no fat at all, but this can be at the expense of their crunchy texture.

> **Stir-frying (in a wok or high-sided skillet):** this method uses a minimum amount of fat without compromising the crunchy texture of the vegetables. But the vegetables cannot be left to cook and have to be stirred continuously. Stir-frying is best done in a wok—not only do the high, curved sides get hot and provide a larger cooking surface, they also allow you to stir the vegetables without splashing the hob.

> **Frying:** This method is fatty, that goes without saying, but deep-fried vegetable fritters are so tasty!

> **Microwaving:** Ideal for boiled vegetables. Cut up the vegetables and place in a dish suitable for microwaving. Add 3 tablespoons water, a little salt and cover. It's quick, the nutritional value of the vegetables is preserved, and the cooking time can be controlled down to the last second—which preserves the vegetables' crunchy texture. Always check the maker's instructions for cooking different vegetables.

> **Roasting or baking:** Arrange the vegetables in an oiled or greased dish, set the oven temperature and your timer and the cooker does the rest. For gratin dishes, the vegetables have to be cooked first before crusting the topping in the oven or under the broiler.

Vegetable	Raw	Boil	Steam	Braise/casserole	Wok/stir fry	Fry	Roast/bake	Micro-wave	Brine	Barbecue
Artichoke	•	•		•	•		•			
Arugula				•						
Asparagus			•							
Avocado	•									
Beansprout	•			•	•					
Beet	•	•				•	•			
Belgian endive	•			•			•			
Bell pepper			•		•		•			
Broad/fava bean	•	•			•					
Cabbage	•	•		•	•			•		
Cardoon		•								
Carrot		•	•	•	•		•			
Celery/celery root		•		•			•			
Chinese artichoke		•		•						
Corn		•	•			•				•
Corn salad	•	•		•						
Cucumber	•				•		•			
Chicory	•									
Eggplant						•				
Fennel	•	•	•	•			•			
French bean		•	•	•	•		•			
Garlic		•		•	•	•	•			
Jerusalem artichoke		•		•			•			
Leek		•		•	•		•	•		
Mushroom	•			•	•					
New Zealand spinach	•									
Onion		•					•			
Pea			•		•					
Pickling cucumbers									•	
Pole bean		•								
Potato		•		•			•			
Pumpkin		•	•	•			•	•		
Radicchio		•		•						
Radish	•	•				•				
Rutabaga		•		•						
Snow peas		•	•	•	•					
Spinach		•		•			•			
Tomato	•			•			•			
Turnip		•	•				•			
Watercress	•									
Zucchini	•	•	•	•	•	•				

	J	F	M	A	M	J	J	A	S	O	N	D
Artichokes				•	••	•••	•••	•••	•••	•••	••	•
Asparagus			•	••	••	••	•					
Avocados	••	•									•	•
Basil	••	••	••	••	•	••	••	••	••	••	••	••
Bay	••	••	••	••	•	••	••	••	••	••	••	••
Beansprouts	••	••	••	••	•	••	••	••	••	••	••	••
Beets	••	••	••	••	•	••	••	••	••	••	••	••
Belgian endive	•••	••	•							•	••	•••
Bell peppers						•	••	••	•			
Broad/fava beans				•	••	••	••	•				
Brussels sprouts	•••	•••	••	•						•	••	•••
Cardoons	••	••	•								•	••
Carrots	••	••	••	••	•	••	••	••	••	••	••	••
Cauliflower	•••	•••	••	•						•	••	•••
Celery	•••	•••	••	•						•	••	•••
Chervil	••	••	••	••	•	••	••	••	••	••	••	••
Chili peppers						•	••	••	•			
Chinese artichokes	••	••	•								•	••
Chinese cabbages	•••	•••	••	•						•	••	•••
Chives	••	••	••	••	•	••	••	••	••	••	••	••
Cilantro	••	••	••	••	•	••	••	••	••	••	••	••
Corn							•	••	••	•		
Cucumbers		•	••	•••	•••	•••	•••	•••	•••	••	•	
Dill	••	••	••	••	•	••	••	••	••	••	••	••
Eggplants						••	•	••				
Fennel	••	••	•								•	••
French/pole beans						••	••	••				
Garlic						••	••					
Green cabbages	•••	•••	••	•						•	••	•••
Jerusalem artichokes	••	••	•								•	••
Leeks	••	••	••	•				•	••		••	••

	j	f	m	a	m	j	j	a	s	o	n	d
Mint	•	•	•	•	•	•	•	•	•	•	•	•
Mushrooms (incl. cèpes, morel, chanterelle)								•	•	•	•	
Onions	•	•	•	•	•	•	•	•	•	•	•	•
Parsley	•	•	•	•	•	•	•	•	•	•	•	•
Peas				•	•	•	•	•				
Pickling cucumbers						•	•	•				
Potatoes (earlies)				•	•	•						
Potatoes (maincrop)	•	•	•	•	•	•	•	•	•	•	•	•
Pumpkins, squashes, gourds	•	•	•						•	•	•	•
Radishes	•	•	•	•	•	•	•	•	•	•	•	•
Red cabbages	•	•	•	•						•	•	•
Romanesco	•	•	•	•						•	•	•
Rosemary	•	•	•	•	•	•	•	•	•	•	•	•
Rutabaga	•	•	•								•	•
Sage	•	•	•	•	•	•	•	•	•	•	•	•
Salad greens	•	•	•	•	•	•	•	•	•	•	•	•
Savory	•	•	•	•	•	•	•	•	•	•	•	•
Shallots	•	•	•	•	•	•	•	•	•	•	•	•
Snow peas				•	•	•	•	•				
Sorrel	•	•	•	•	•	•	•	•	•	•	•	•
Spinach	•	•	•	•	•	•	•	•	•	•	•	•
Tarragon	•	•	•	•	•	•	•	•	•	•	•	•
Thyme	•	•	•	•	•	•	•	•	•	•	•	•
Tomatoes					•	•	•	•	•	•		
Turnips	•	•	•								•	•
Watercress						•	•	•	•	•	•	
Zucchini						•	•	•	•			

INDEX OF RECIPES

The author would like to thank:

Isabelle Cavillac, 198 rue Mouneyra, 33000 Bordeaux, and Marché Munipal Cap-Ferret: *Chez Cocotte, 'la reine du melon sucré'*, a connoisseur who sells the very best fruit and vegetables from all over France.

Hélène L, a top cook who, although not a great fan of vegetables, kindly agreed to try out some of my recipes—and has been a devotee ever since.

My chef friends, **Yves Camdeborde** (*La Régalade*), **Thierry Breton** (*Chez Michel*), **Thierry Faucher** (*L'Os à Moelle*), **Rodophe Paquin** (*Le Repaire de Cartouche*) and **Éric Frechon** (*Hôtel du Bristol*), who allowed me into their kitchens and taught me so much.

The editor would like to thank Laurence Denavit and Gaëlle Moreno for their invaluable help.

Photo credits
All photographs were taken by **Patrick Bauer**, with the exception of those on pages: 15 (top left), 19 (top right), 37 (top right), 55 (bottom right), 69 (top right), 111 (top right), 135 (left), 143 (bottom), 145 (left), 146 (right)—Iris Sullivan; 23 (top right), 65 (top right), 97 (bottom), 103 (bottom), 147, 151 (bottom)—Jean-Blaise Hall; 59 (bottom right), 145 (right), 146 (left), 151 (top)—Pierre Desgrieux.

Director: Stephen Bateman
Editor: Pierre-Jean Furet
Proofreading: Anne la Fay
Editorial office: Marine Barbier-Blin
Graphics: Gérard Piassale
Design and layout: Anne Schlaffmann